The Dilemma of Divorced Catholics

Where Do You Stand with the Church?
What Is the Internal Forum?

THE DILEMMA OF DIVORCED CATHOLICS

Where Do You Stand with the Church?
What Is the Internal Forum?

(Revised Edition)

John T. Catoir, JCD

Resurrection Press
An Imprint of
CATHOLIC BOOK PUBLISHING CORP.
Totowa • New Jersey

Revised Edition published in April 2007 by
Catholic Book Publishing/Resurrection Press
77 West End Road
Totowa, NJ 07512

Previously published by the Society of St. Paul

Copyright © 2007 by John T. Catoir, JCD

ISBN 978-1-933066-06-6

Library of Congress Catalog Card Number: 2007921101

Cover design by Beth DeNapoli

Printed in the United States of America

1 2 3 4 5 6 7 8 9

www.catholicbookpublishing.com

Contents

Introduction   7

Chapter 1: Where Do You Stand with the Church?   11

Chapter 2: Why is the Church So Strict on Marriage?   21

Chapter 3: What is a Church Annulment?   39

Chapter 4: What is the Internal Forum?   69

Chapter 5: Where Does the Church Stand with You?   99

Introduction

NEARLY forty years ago Father John Reedy called me to do an interview with him for the bimonthly newsletter, *A.D. Correspondence*. At that time I had been the Judicial Vicar of the Marriage Tribunal for about ten years in the Diocese of Paterson, New Jersey, and he wanted my views on the evolving picture of marriage and divorce in the Catholic Church. I did the interview and eventually expanded it into a book for Ave Maria Press. It sold over 35,000 copies in the first two years.

The book you are now reading is an updated version of that original publication. It incorporates material from the revised *Code of Canon Law* and the *Catechism of the Catholic Church*. My aim is to offer encouragement to those who are experiencing the pain of a broken marriage.

I lived and worked through much of the evolution that took place in our marriage tribunals over the past forty years. I have a doctorate in canon law, and until recently I served as a judge in the Paterson Court of Second Instance.

From 1978 to 1995, I was the director of The Christophers, a multi-media organization based in New York City. In that capacity I interacted with a vast audience of people who were wounded by the trials of modern life. The soaring divorce rate reflected the strains and stresses of married life.

When I first started working in the marriage tribunal in the early 1960s, annulments were quite rare. Cases required proof positive and the grounds for an annulment were severely limited. The tradition was more legalistic than pastoral. I won't bore you with details, but the law often frustrated tribunal judges who felt a pastoral concern for the couples involved.

It took years of struggle on the part of the Canon Law Society of America to convince the hierarchy that our tribunal system needed reform. Eventually, the bishops agreed, and they brought the issue to Pope Paul VI, who granted 23 experimental procedural norms to remedy the situation. Many of these reforms found their way into the revised *Code of Canon Law* published in 1983.

I have tried to express my compassion for people in marital difficulty while at the same time remaining faithful to the Church's teaching. Marriage is an indissoluble bond. I respect the teaching authority of the Church and submit to that authority in complete peace.

The question before every church tribunal is this: Which of the marriages presented for an annulment are truly valid, and which are not? No one questions the fact that marriage is indissoluble, and that a truly valid marriage bond cannot be broken or dissolved, and that no one can validly begin a new marriage while an existing valid marriage is still in possession, but we can and must ask questions if a serious doubt exists concerning the validity of a specific marriage.

The *Letter to the Bishops of the Catholic Church Concerning the Reception of Holy Communion by Divorced and Remarried Members of the Faithful* issued by the Congregation for the Doctrine of the Faith (Sept. 14, 1994) is an authoritative document which accurately reflects the teachings of the

1980 Synod of Bishops, and of Pope John Paul II in his Apostolic Exhortation *Familiaris Consortio*. This teaching is based on the presumption that the first marriage is valid. If there is doubt about that validity, we have the marriage tribunal to resolve it. The principle of indissolubility is unchanging, but the application of the law to the facts will differ with each particular case.

Sometimes people cannot get an annulment even after trying for years. Many of them, believing they have sound reasons for doubting the validity of the marriage in question, end up following their consciences and marrying again, outside the Church. This is often referred to as an internal forum solution.

St. Paul's pastoral statement to the Galatians put the whole issue in perspective, "Help carry one another's burdens, in that way you will fulfill the law of Jesus Christ" (Gal 6:2). Ever since I read that line, I have understood clearly that the defense of all our legal principles must be done within the context of the supreme law of charity. St. Augustine said, "Do what you can do, and pray for what you cannot yet do." Many good people have followed St. Augustine's advice.

I am indebted to all those who helped me prepare this manuscript, and I offer this book with love to everyone in need. May the Lord be your strength and your joy.

—Father John T. Catoir

CHAPTER 1

Where Do You Stand with the Church?

IN many dioceses throughout the country parishes run a "Come Home" program for lapsed Catholics. They advertise a series of information meetings, and usually attract a large turnout. At the first meeting, participants make a list of questions and concerns. Then a variety of workshops are offered to address those topics. Most of the questions raised have to do with Church laws concerning marriage and divorce. Here are a few of the questions and answers that have come out of these sessions:

I have doubts about the Immaculate Conception and the Assumption. Can I still be Catholic?

Doubts are a normal part of a person's faith life. If you are open-minded in dealing with doubts, it can lead to a deepening of your faith. You can go to the workshop on resolving doubts for more information.

Can someone who has had an abortion reconcile with the Church?

Yes, through the sacrament of Reconciliation (Confession). For additional information see the Project Rachel brochure.

I am divorced. Does that mean I am excommunicated?

No, you are not excommunicated. You're still a Catholic. Some very holy people had to separate from their spouses for reasons beyond their control. They remained practicing Catholics. Dorothy Day, who is being considered for sainthood, had to leave her common-law husband. She was struggling to raise her daughter at the same time she started the Catholic Worker movement. Catherine de Hueck Doherty, the founder of Madonna House in Canada, left her first husband after years of emotional abuse, and entered into a second marriage after obtaining an annulment. She is also being considered for canonization.

As a divorced Catholic, may I receive Holy Communion?

Yes. A divorced Catholic who has not remarried outside the Church may continue to receive Holy Communion.

But can I receive Communion if I remarried outside the Church? I feel my second marriage is okay with God, but not with the Church.

You don't give enough information for a completely accurate answer. We suggest that you attend the workshops on annulments and the internal forum (more on the internal forum in chapter 4).

I was a Godparent when I was still in good standing in the Church. Now I am divorced and remarried outside the Church. What about my responsibility as a Godparent?

Your responsibility as a Godparent does not change.

How can a divorced non-Catholic join the Church?

If you are willing to undertake a form of life consistent with the Church's teaching on the indissolubility of marriage, any priest can help you enroll in the RCIA program (Rite of Christian Initiation for Adults). This program invites you to join a Catholic worshipping community of your choice. You would be most welcome.

* * *

The most compelling question asked by divorced Catholics at these "Come Home" sessions is: *Where do I stand with the Church?* It is a question that evokes much emotional pain, and one that is impossible to answer in a general way. Certain guidelines may be of help. First let me dispel a few of the myths that cause needless confusion.

The following statements are all FALSE:

Divorced Catholics who have not remarried . . .

- are automatically excommunicated
- can no longer consider themselves Catholics
- are in the state of permanent mortal sin
- may not serve as sponsors at Baptism or Confirmation
- may not receive the sacraments of Eucharist or Penance
- are not allowed Christian burial in the Catholic Church

The following are also FALSE statements.

Divorced Catholics who have remarried without an annulment . . .

- are automatically excommunicated
- may not attend Mass and are not welcome at parish activities
- may not receive the sacrament of Reconciliation
- should no longer consider themselves Catholic
- may not have their children baptized or confirmed in a Catholic Church
- are not allowed Christian burial in the Catholic Church

Marriage Tribunals in the Catholic Church

- consider the children from annulled marriages to be illegitimate
- require you to pay exorbitant fees for an annulment
- only grant annulments to people with power and influence
- refuse annulments to people who were married a long time
- refuse annulments to people with children
- take many years to process even the simplest case

If you're surprised that all of these statements are FALSE, you're not alone. The number of people who stay away from the sacraments because of incorrect information is astounding. One man wept when he was told there was no barrier between himself and God. A woman, who came back to the sacraments after four years, was filled with joy and gratitude. "Truly having God in my life once again is the greatest gift anyone could have been given."

Where do you stand with the Church? It depends on your situation, but chances are you're in better shape than you think. Remember, God is unchanging Love. That means he loves you!

The important thing to keep in mind is that Jesus came to seek out all those who are lost. The very fact that you're reading this book speaks volumes about the grace of God working in you.

The Church is a refuge for sinners, and who among us is without sin? Think more about the divine element of the Church and less about the human element. You'll be on the right track if you remember that God's mercy is infinite.

In this book I have tried to answer the questions that are most frequently asked about divorce, remarriage and annulments. There is so much spiritual and emotional pain connected with the failure of marriages. Divorce is one of the great tragedies of modern life. When you cannot get your first marriage to work in spite of your best efforts, and you realize that reconciliation is no longer possible, it's time to rebuild your life. The Church is the carrier of God's love, and it has a responsibility to minister to the many victims of broken dreams.

There is no greater source of solace than the knowledge of God's love. As more and more divorced Catholics remarry without the benefit of an annulment, they come to wonder: *Does God still love me? Am I living in sin? How can I resume my life as an active Catholic? How can I participate in the sacramental life of the Church?* Be patient and don't give up hope.

If a divorced Catholic obtains an annulment and has the new marriage validated in the Church, everything is fine, but what about those who have simply followed their consciences and acted as if they have God's blessing on their second marriage? If there is no annulment, they have a canonical problem and possibly a grave moral problem.

Church leaders are exploring new ways to offer pastoral care to divorced and remarried Catholics by attempting to discern the truth in each case. In 1995, for example, Bishop Karl Lehmann of Mainz, the president of the German Bishops' Conference and a respected theologian, called for an open debate on this subject. In doing so, he challenged a ruling of the Holy See. The story is an interesting one.

Bishop Lehmann and two other German bishops were permitting some couples in non-canonical or invalid marriages to receive the Eucharist. They investigated each marriage on a case by case basis. If the couple had grounds for believing that an earlier marriage was invalid, the bishops, after examining the facts resolved the doubt in some cases by giving the couple permission to receive the Eucharist. By doing this, they circumvented the tribunal process, and thereby created a procedure which was contrary to canon law.

This action was like writing a new law. Rome immediately objected to the practice because the pope is the sole legislator for the Church. Had the Holy See said nothing, the silence would have implied consent. Legally, the German bishops had no right to invent a new procedure. The issue had a lot more to do with the question of who can write new laws for the Church than it did with pastoral solutions, but it demonstrates the fact that this is not a closed issue.

Once challenged, the German bishops immediately stopped the practice of allowing certain Catholics in non-canonical marriages to receive Holy Communion. However, Bishop Lehmann also called for further debate, sending the message to Rome that serious dissatisfaction exists with the present system because the truth about a particular couple's standing before God cannot always be resolved satisfactorily by our current legal process.

It is interesting to note that in preventing the German bishops from invoking this external forum solution, the Holy See made no mention of the internal forum. The internal forum deals with people's consciences, not with external procedures. However, the internal forum also has to do with the pursuit of truth. It is a discernment process, which is resolved within the privacy of one's conscience and often with the help of a prudent confessor (cf. chapter 4).

Marriage tribunals are basically courts of law. A marriage case is not heard before a jury, but a panel of three judges. Usually, the couple never sees the judges. They simply give their testimony in a private interview. The judges study the records of the case and make their decision on the basis of the evidence presented to them. If the tribunal refuses to hear a case or if it renders a decision which the couple thinks is unfair, they can appeal it.

When *all* legal remedies are exhausted, and the couple believes an injustice has been done, the only remaining resource is the internal forum. Many people in so-called "invalid marriages" may decide to continue receiving Holy Communion because of their deep conviction that they are in the state of grace. This takes great courage, and they will have to answer to God for their actions, but if they are clear about it, the priests will respect their conscience.

No generalizations can be made in these matters since all cases differ, but some non-canonical marriages definitely qualify as "good conscience marriages." A priest confessor does not have authority to give permission to any couple to live in a non-canonical marriage, but he can listen to their story, and help them discern if they have reasonable grounds for believing that they are not living in sin. In doing so, the priest is not playing God; he is merely respecting their conscientious decision.

You may be interested to know that the Holy See has a department called the Sacred Penitentiary which deals exclusively with matters involving the internal forum. A commentary on canon 64 in the Code of Canon Law reads: **The competence of the Sacred Penitentiary "comprises all things which concern the internal forum . . ."**

Very little is known about the work of the Sacred Penitentiary because it is entirely confidential in nature, but you should be aware that the internal forum is acknowledged within the Church and in the *Code of Canon Law*. However, you do not need to petition the Holy See to follow your conscience.

Today's tribunals are more efficient than ever before, but they are still far from perfect. Because mistakes are made, we cannot rule out the right of individuals to follow their own consciences. Conscientious discernment on the part of married couples is not only a right, but a duty.

In a matter as serious as the natural right to marry, we have to respect people's right to follow their consciences. They also have a duty to form their consciences in the light of objective truth and God's law. To do this they do not need a degree in canon law.

Over the years, it has become evident that in certain marriages the legal presumption of validity has worked harshly and at times incorrectly. Marriages that are total disasters from day one are nevertheless presumed to be valid until the contrary is proven. This is logical from the point of view of public order, but it is not reasonable if it flies in the face of truth. When the letter of the law works against the truth, couples have to seek the help of the Church and if necessary follow their consciences. The big question is: What is the truth? Before God what is your true relationship to the other person? Was the original contract valid?

In the following chapters, I will explain why the Church is so tough in handling marriage cases. At the same time, I'll try to offer hope to those in need. The Church has the duty to be strict in these matters to protect the common good, but it must also be full of mercy and compassion in the process.

CHAPTER 2

Why is the Church So Strict on Marriage?

THE Church is demanding when it comes to marriage in order to be faithful to Jesus Christ. He taught us that a true marriage is indissoluble. Marriage is the sacred commitment of two people, who bind themselves to one another for life. When a person makes a public vow before God, he or she does not have the arbitrary right to revoke it at will. The Church respects you enough to take you at your word and to hold you to your vows.

All the major religions of the world encourage fidelity in marriage. The Catholic Church takes it one step further by making marriage a sacrament. Canon 1055 states:

> The matrimonial covenant by which a man and a woman establish between themselves a partnership of the whole of life, is by its nature ordered toward the good of the spouses and the procreation and education of offspring; this covenant between baptized persons has been raised by Christ the Lord to the dignity of a sacrament.

For this reason a matrimonial contract cannot validly exist between baptized persons unless it is also a sacrament by that fact.

Not everyone is psychologically capable of making such a commitment, even though they might say the right words. Psychological incapacity might be hidden from our eyes on the wedding day, but sooner or later the impediment will come to light. Obviously the Church has to be careful about who it allows to receive the sacrament of Matrimony. But in spite of careful scrutiny, some bad ones get through. There's another less obvious reason why the Church is so strict. We are trying to defend women against abuse. Throughout history, men have treated their wives like chattel, and discarded them at will. In today's world, some women discard their husbands as well.

The trivialization of marriage is wrong no matter who is responsible. Jesus called marriage an indissoluble union. He forbade divorce not only to protect women against man's polygamous nature, but to stabilize family life. "What therefore God has joined together, let no man put asunder" (Mt 19:6-8). To disregard this teaching is immoral.

Unfortunately, not every couple who marries has what it takes to make a life-long commitment. Today's divorce statistics indicate that many couples lack the necessary maturity and the moral resolve needed for a truly valid marriage.

Neil Clark Warren, a psychologist and marriage counselor, estimates that in 75% of all divorces at least one marriage partner is emotionally unhealthy. Obviously, a person is incapable of marrying if he or she is mentally sick.

We can't always detect mental illness in advance. I remember one of my earliest marriage cases as a parish priest. When the couple came for prenuptial instructions, I noticed the man never looked me in the eye. I attributed it to shyness. Thirty days after the wedding his young wife showed up at my door crying. Her husband was behaving in the most obnoxious manner, continually throwing tantrums when he didn't get his way. At one point, he even urinated in her bureau drawer to get even with her for some trivial annoyance. He was a certifiable mental case, but prior to the marriage no one had spotted the severity of his mental condition. His capacity for a true love relationship was severely limited at the time of the marriage. She eventually got an annulment because he had concealed his prior psychiatric history from her.

The Church tries to reduce these mistakes to a minimum by requiring couples to complete a premarital questionnaire. If true freedom is not present when the vows are exchanged, there is no marriage. If they do not want to have any children or if they do not agree to enter a truly permanent union, a priest would not allow them to marry in the Catholic Church. The nature of marriage is not something the parties can define for themselves. There are objective norms that must be verified. The parties to a Catholic marriage must agree on the essential elements of marriage.

The Rising Divorce Rate

In modern times there are many disturbing reasons for a tough policy on marriage. Recent studies show that divorce often creates many more problems than it solves:

- Divorce contributes to as many as 3 out of every 4 teen suicides, and 4 out of 5 teen psychiatric admissions.
- Children of divorce are much more likely to drop out of school, have premarital sex and become pregnant outside of marriage than those in intact families.
- Young adults (18-22) from divorced families are twice as likely to have poor relationships with parents and show high levels of emotional distress as young adults from intact families.
- The remarriage of parents does not protect their children from behavioral and other problems.

Even though the Church has taken a strong stand against divorce, our culture has trivialized sexuality to such a degree over the past fifty years that the institution of marriage itself has become devalued.

In the last forty years, the divorce rate has more than doubled, which means that the number of divorced adults has quadrupled. Statistics show that family instability has become the dominant sociological characteristic of our time. Today, nearly half of all children do not live with two parents. In 1960, nine out of ten children did.

More disturbing is the fact that divorce has become so acceptable even in marriages where there are children. The proportion of those who *disagreed* with this statement—"When there are children in the family, parents should stay together even if they don't get along"—grew from 51% in 1962, to an astounding 90% in 2006. This means that most adults believe that children should not get in the way of a parent's right to self-fulfillment, even if it means divorce. Only a small percentage of all parents believe that the needs of their children should deter parents from breaking up.

When most parents put themselves before the well-being of their children, it does not bode well for the future of our society.

It is difficult to estimate the effect that divorce will have on the character of the American people in the long run. Some have said our nation is dying a slow death. If that's true, we're not alone. All the major industrial nations of the world have a soaring divorce rate. That fact doesn't offer much solace; it only tells us the problem is widespread. Sociologists differ widely on the meaning of it all, but one thing is certain: everyone suffers when there is a divorce. That is why the Church tries so hard to help people to do their very best to make their marriage work.

If you are in an unhappy marriage and are contemplating divorce, please think long and hard about it. You'll need to deepen your spiritual life and turn to God for help. A lot of people are coming to the conclusion that it's infinitely better to go for counseling than to discard the marriage.

Getting a divorce should be much harder when children are involved. Children bear the brunt of a failed marriage. But it is also true that children suffer when they are being raised in a dysfunctional family. They bear the brunt of living in a war zone. Sometimes a divorce is necessary to protect the children. Nevertheless, divorce is such a serious step, both parents must try to weigh the consequences.

I remember the case of a six-year-old boy who blamed himself for his parents' break up. He was in therapy for depression for many years because he had spilled his milk one morning. The accident precipitated a shouting match between his parents and when they separated a few days later, the child thought the incident of the spilled milk was the cause of their breakup. It took years to assure him that he was not to blame for the divorce.

It's not surprising that the first generation of those raised under "no-fault" divorce laws has already started to demand tougher divorce codes. They have seen the havoc caused by a permissive society. One young woman wrote a letter to the editor: "A marriage is a contract. Breaching that contract doesn't automatically ensure financial ruin (like a business) or cause violence or possible death (like poor military leadership). Its results are far worse. Family infighting, misguided children, separation, forced visitation, guilt-ridden children—the list could go on . . . Bad marriages exist because of selfish marriers." She therefore concludes, *"make divorce very hard."*

Certainly, the pressures of the modern world are more intense than in former generations. The moral atmosphere in this country has deteriorated to the point where sexual promiscuity and infidelity are routine in many circles. The corporate world puts great demands on employees today. Business trips are necessary and frequent, but they are often the cause of serious temptations. The traveling spouse is alone in a distant city; the spouse who is left alone at home often feels abandoned. There's a lot of room for human weakness to take over.

Modern technology has also introduced an assortment of new temptations. There are things happening on the Internet that earlier generations never imagined. A rendezvous in cyberspace, computer to computer, can turn into a red-hot extramarital affair conducted entirely by way of e-mail. All of this whittles away the fabric of family life.

It has become less desirable to start a family and raise children because the need for mobility and flexibility is essential in today's job market. Years ago, only military personnel and a few others were subject to the stress of constant relocation. Now nearly every professional man or woman who works for a large corporation must be willing to move when the company dictates.

The nature of contemporary family life itself creates problems. Once upon a time the family unit provided its own life support system. The home was once the center of every activity. Today, school, work, sports activities, socializing, and even most eating takes place outside the home. It is estimated that more than one half of the meals in America are eaten in restaurants, mostly of the fast food variety.

Too often, children are left unsupervised for hours in front of a television set. Teenagers watching mindless television sitcoms, grow up believing that sex is a form of recreation. It isn't until later in life that they come to see the terrible pain and misery caused by promiscuity and marital infidelity.

With everyone in the family moving in a different direction, people don't have time to listen to one another as much as they used to, and sometimes, they simply stop caring about one another.

The number of natural, nuclear families is also declining. Legal kinships, built on relationships through adoption and remarriage, are on the increase. The U.S. Census Bureau reported that the number of step-families increased 36% between 1980 and 1990 to a total of 5.3 million. Twenty-one percent of all married couples with dependent children were in step-families. These numbers have almost doubled since then.

Unfortunately, a happier remarried mom or dad does not always translate into contented kids, according to David Blankenhorn, author of *Fatherless America*. The economic advantages of remarriage are often offset by the rivalry of step-children born of different marriages. These are the facts of modern life.

All of which shows how important it is to persevere in a difficult marriage if at all possible.

The Root of the Problem: Unrealistic Expectations

Most people think of marriage as a path toward self-fulfillment, and why not? Isn't everyone seeking human happiness? Yet, if you choose a marriage partner on the basis of companionship alone without much thought given to the larger picture of character and family life, you may be disappointed. Romantic feelings evaporate in time. Unless there is a sense of commitment and a determination to remain faithful to one's vows, the marriage can deteriorate. A good marriage requires a strong spiritual life.

Surely a person has a right to hope for self-fulfillment in a happy marriage, but this cannot be achieved without sacrifice. This is why the challenge of a happy marriage is essentially a spiritual one. Unfortunately, God's will is seldom considered in these crisis situations.

"To sacrifice" is to give up a legitimate good for some higher purpose. Married people sacrifice their freedom in order to create a life in common. Performing one's duties in life is an important part of human success. The idea of delayed gratification is no longer popular. Generally speaking, today's young adults want instant gratification. Many of the Baby Boomers, those born between 1946 and 1964, tended to think in terms of the happiness of the moment. This has been intensified in their children and grandchildren.

One of the great spiritual writers of the seventeenth century, Father Jean Pierre de Caussade, S.J., wrote a book entitled *Abandonment to Divine Providence,* in which he said, "The secret of holiness and happiness is found in fidelity to the will of God as it is manifested in the duty of the present moment."

Duty and honor should be more valued than selfish desire. It takes two people with spiritual values working together to save a faltering marriage.

A marriage can work if both parties are faithful to one another and to their children day by day. It takes prayer to maintain the will to persevere. It takes spiritual discipline to keep asking yourself, "What does God want of me in this situation?" Swallowing your pride may be what God is asking of you at this moment. Tensions can reach a boiling point and you may need couple's counseling at times, but don't give up too easily!

Sometimes people want to break up amicably, but when a lawyer enters the picture, things change. A man from Massachusetts writes: "Not wanting to end up in a bitter battle, we sought the advice of an independent divorce attorney. Both of us had agreed to go by the numbers he put forth, regardless. Within 10 minutes he had dragged us into a fighting, screaming, acrimonious divorce over everything but child support that ran on and on until our five-year-old son was almost 9 years old . . . It took us until he was 18 to actually speak civilly to one another." When a divorce is absolutely certain, using a divorce mediator can often soften the painful experience.

Making the necessary sacrifices to avoid this kind of pain is worth the effort. Eating humble pie might be a good thing for all concerned in the long run. However, doing what is necessary to make the marriage work is even better.

Some marriages could be saved simply by making a commitment to fidelity. When people consider infidelity as only a minor indiscretion, they are dead wrong. They risk becoming emotionally involved with another person and growing cold to their marriage partner. What a cruel blow to a spouse who has honestly given trust and love, and what an injustice to the children if it leads to a break-up.

A married woman once told me in confidence that she would wake up in a cold sweat saying, "I'm seducing him. I'm seducing him." She was being sweet and flirtatious with a man at work. It was all innocent enough because no physical contact had yet been made, but she knew what she was doing. In the deep recesses of her conscience she was disturbed by her behavior. She would wake up in a cold sweat because she knew that this could actually end up in adultery. She really cared about her family and didn't want to put them at risk so she resolved to monitor her behavior. It took her subconscious mind in a dream to help her see the deeper implications of her human desires. Bravo!

Making sacrifices takes great courage. Sometimes people try heroically to save their marriages, but find that nothing works. It takes two to achieve the ideal of permanence in marriage. If one party is determined to destroy the marriage, the other party is virtually helpless. I know of a man whose wife left him after he was diagnosed with multiple sclerosis. She said she couldn't handle his illness and didn't want that kind of a life. It broke his heart. One wonders what kind of woman would do such a thing to the man she once loved. The same kind of thing happens in marriages when the wife suffers a physical or emotional setback. The husband is often unable to handle the burden of sickness—even when it is temporary.

In some cases, a divorce is inevitable when the abuse becomes intolerable. I dealt with a case where the husband never asked for sex. When the wife tried to initiate it, he rebuffed her saying that her amorous advances only turned him off. For years, she felt unattractive and defective. Only later did she discover that he was an active homosexual. A cruel deceit!

There are situations where a person has a moral obligation to walk out. I will never forget the case of a wife-abuser. He was a respected public official, who abused his wife both psychologically and physically. To the world he was a man of impeccable credentials, but at home he was a monster. After he would abuse her, he would beg for forgiveness, but he never kept his word. The cycle of violence was always repeated. When she finally broke the code of secrecy that he imposed and reported him to the police, he was publicly humiliated. He stopped the physical abuse, but the marriage soured even more because of his resentment. She eventually left him.

Each case is unique. Some people must separate, but others need to try harder. In most cases, the marriage would improve if the couple put God's will before their own. God doesn't ask anyone to become a doormat, but he does call spouses to make sacrifices for the good of others. We have to get back to God's plan for us. *Romantic love withers and dies, but true love is a commitment that endures the storms of life.*

During the years I was in charge of the marriage tribunal, the wife of a successful professional man came in seeking an annulment. She was convinced her husband didn't love her. After she told me her story, I asked her two questions:

"Do you love your husband?"

"Yes," she replied. "At least I have up until now."

"Does he love you?"

"No, I don't think so," she said.

Later I met privately with the husband, and after he told his side of the story, I asked him the same questions:

"Do you love your wife?"

"Of course, I love my wife!" he insisted.

"Does your wife love you?"

"Yes," he said, "I know she loves me."

The husband was blind to his wife's feelings. Their love was still alive, but they had a communication problem.

The wife was not sure of her husband's love. He was so dedicated to his job—she felt deserted. The money he gave her was no substitute for emotional support. She harbored many bitter memories. One of their children was born when he was away on business. She was certain that he could have been with her if he really cared. From that time on, she began to feel that he didn't really love her any more. She never discussed her feelings and they began to fester. Finally, she pushed him for a show-down: "Either you change your work habits, or I will leave you."

Furious at being handed what he considered a ridiculous ultimatum, he refused. At that point, she came to see me about an annulment. She really didn't want a divorce, so instead of going to a lawyer she came to me.

I made a strong effort to reconcile them by encouraging her to be more assertive in expressing her need for attention, and persuading him to stop taking her for granted. It worked. They both made concessions and the marriage is doing much better.

Sometimes, a third party, especially a marriage counselor, can make a difference. Many divorced people later wish they had tried harder to reconcile.

If your marriage is floundering, go for help! Every new car comes with a manufacturer's manual telling you how to maintain it. You'd be a fool to throw away that manual. Forgetting to add oil can only lead to a serious breakdown. Human life is like that. It needs care and maintenance. We need to follow God's plan if we are to have a happy life. A counselor can often point the couple in the right direction.

Marriage is difficult, but "Love can make it easy and perfect love can make it a joy." That's a line from the

Catholic Church's marriage ritual. Love involves service and sacrifice, but perfect love is the laying down of one's ego. Long-standing marriages exist because both partners want to stay married. They sustain this intention through prayer, sacrifice and hard work. To succeed you'll need God's grace. Pray for the grace to do each day what God would want you to do.

At a fiftieth anniversary party I sat chatting with the good Italian wife, who was enjoying the day immensely. "Between you and me Father," she confided. "I left him for a while when we were about ten years married. He was running around and I couldn't take it. He came to me after a year or so, and begged me to take him back. I'm so glad I did because we've had many good years since then."

Every marriage has its ups and downs. It takes a lot of forgiveness and humility to get through the dark times. If you know how to say you're sorry, you'll have a better chance at happiness.

Forgiveness is not necessarily a matter of having good feelings toward the person who hurt you. Those feelings have a life of their own. They won't disappear on command.

True forgiveness is in the will. The will says yes or no. If you decide to forgive, don't wait for your feelings to catch up. Just say, "Yes. I forgive." Forgive because the Lord asks it of you. Do it for the sake of the marriage—even if your spouse doesn't deserve it. Your feelings will not cooperate at first, but in time they will fall in line. Feelings follow thoughts. If you will to forgive, God will supply the grace, and peace of mind will return eventually.

If you are planning to remarry, you should be aware that over 60% of second marriages fail. Why? Because people often come to the second marriage without having figured out the reasons that caused their first marriage to fail.

For instance, if a person still believes that romantic love is the essence of a happy marriage, they are apt to repeat the same mistake. When passions start to cool off, they give up. Some people spend their entire lives chasing romantic feelings, but feelings do not necessarily indicate a true love commitment. When romance fades, the marriage will go on only if you will it.

Husbands and wives have bad feelings toward one another from time to time, but the love commitment can transcend feelings. Good, warm feelings return in time, but if there is no commitment, no spiritual depth, the couple will drift apart before they get their second wind. True, lasting love is in the will.

Can a person live happily without romantic love? Of course. In many cultures marriages are arranged by the parents. It is immaterial if the couple feels any attraction to one another. They are told that love will come after the second child. I do not advocate a return to arranged marriages, but I find it interesting that countless men and women over the centuries entered arranged marriages and succeeded. They learned to love their mate without the benefit of romantic love. Surprisingly, the overall divorce rate in these countries is much lower than our own.

These marriages last because the couples make a commitment to stay in a permanent union. Romantic feelings come and go at various stages of life, but real love endures. A commitment to stand by your spouse in good times and in bad is a thing of beauty. It takes discipline, and the will to bear discomfort. It takes a vow before God to make it work.

Another hint if you're starting out a second time: try to accept yourself, warts and all. Self-acceptance is the basis of all personal growth. Loving yourself is essential for spiritual growth. If you cannot accept your own faults and failings, how can you accept the imperfections of your spouse? If you're a perfectionist or a controller, please go for counseling.

The adult children of alcoholics and others who grew up in dysfunctional families often feel they must control everyone around them. A controller must learn to let go and trust more. Change may take a long time to achieve, but it can be done.

A happy marriage requires work. The management of time and money requires certain skills. Effective communication is also important. Developing the will to cope with stress, boredom and difficulties of all kinds, and a willingness to share responsibilities can help lighten the burdens of life. All of these skills can be learned. Go for help. Study together. You can realize your full potential, if you work at it. Also, a sense of humor is vital. We have to laugh at ourselves more.

Learning about the psychology of the opposite sex can also go a long way toward preparing couples for problems that arise in close personal relationships. The ability to love can be nurtured by a greater awareness of the motives of your spouse.

For those considering marriage, learn more about the way men and women speak to one another. Sometimes they use the same words, but the words contain different meanings. Talk about your ideas on child-rearing and finances. Do you agree on having children? How will you deal with your in-laws? Have you discussed your feelings about religion? This is especially important in an inter-faith marriage. How and where will you celebrate holidays? In what areas of life are you willing to bend and in what areas would you resist? Would you be willing to give up your job if your spouse got a fabulous position in another city? A good marriage requires open, honest communication.

I advise people not to marry until they are willing to accept the real burdens of a life shared in common. A couple needs maturity, moral character and a strong commitment to maintain a successful marriage, and it really helps when you're truly in love. Living together prior to marriage is not advised because it leaves the back door open. Marriage, above all, is a commitment, not an experiment.

Matrimony is the sacrament which consecrates human love. It is holy before the Lord. For that reason it takes three to stay married: you, your spouse and Almighty God.

CHAPTER 3

What is a Church Annulment?

A N ecclesiastical annulment is a declaration that a marriage, which at first appeared to be valid, was canonically defective in some way from the beginning. When an annulment is granted, the Church recognizes that all the children born of the marriage are legitimate. An illegitimate child is one born out of wedlock.

The Church always sets out to follow Christ's teaching: "What therefore God has joined together, let no man put asunder" (Mt 19:6-8). In an annulment case, the question put before the Church tribunal is this: Is God really the author of this union? If the answer is yes, we cannot tamper with the marriage. If the answer is no, the marriage should not be presumed to be valid (cf. *Code of Canon Law*, Canon 1057 #1).

If it is clear that this is not a canonically valid marriage, the Church not only has the right, but the duty to annul it. What appears to be a valid marriage is not always so. Sometimes circumstances exist which are not obvious to the average person. Sometimes there is an element of fraud or psychological incapacity present. It's a matter of justice to help the party who was defrauded or deceived to be free to marry again.

To protect against fraud, the Church requires that each party sign a pre-marital form indicating that they intend to be faithful to one another for life; that they intend to have children; and that they are both free to enter into this union. If it can be proven that either party did not tell the truth, knowingly or unknowingly, the marriage can be formally nullified.

If true consent is lacking, the contract is invalid. The consent must be a free human act of the will by which "the partners mutually give themselves to each other."

The Church requires a lot of paperwork before the marriage because people can deceive themselves and one another wittingly or unwittingly. To protect against mistakes the Church asks a lot of questions.

When a Catholic marries outside the Church either before a civil authority or a non-Catholic minister, it is called a "Defect of Form" marriage, and it can be declared null. Canon law requires that Catholics marry in the Church.

What are the grounds for an annulment?

If you are trying to discern the validity of your marriage, ask yourself these questions:

- Were you pressured to marry by your parents or your spouse's parents for any reason like an unexpected pregnancy for example?
- Did your spouse marry to conceal a homosexual orientation?
- Did you find out after years of humiliation that your spouse was an alcoholic with no intention of getting help and lacked the necessary freedom to make a commitment?

- Did you discover that your spouse was incapable of sexual fidelity?
- Did the marriage break up because of physical or psychological difficulties?
- Did your husband or wife conceal a history of psychological problems?
- At the time of the wedding, did your spouse intend to stay with you only for a limited period?
- Did either one of you refuse to have children?
- Did you marry before a justice of the peace?*
- Was your spouse married to someone else at any time prior to your marriage without telling you?

* A Catholic cannot validly marry outside of the Church (cf. *Code of Canon Law,* Canon 1057 #2).

A Catholic Church annulment is an authoritative, judicial declaration that the marriage bond did not come into existence at the time the marriage vows were exchanged because some essential property of a true marriage was missing. God did not join the man and woman together. An annulment is simply the outcome of a legal process in which human judges consider the evidence presented and make a ruling. There is nothing magical about it.

What is the basis of a sacramental marriage?

When two baptized Catholics freely marry, it is a sacrament. The marriage contract is the sacrament. The priest acts as a necessary, qualified witness, but the two parties confer the sacrament upon one another. They are the ministers of the sacrament.

The matter and form of the sacrament of Matrimony is the mutual giving and receiving of consent. This consent is a pledge to love, care for, and be faithful to one's spouse. The sacrament therefore is the consecration of human love expressed in a mutual commitment.

In an annulment, the Church formally declares that there never was a true Catholic marriage in the canonical sense. *The annulment is not dissolving what God has joined together, it is merely recognizing that a true marriage bond never came into existence.*

What does the Church have to say about the purpose of marriage?

According to canon law, marriage is a permanent society between a man and a woman for the purpose of procreating children. The Second Vatican Council refined this teaching by emphasizing the importance of the mutual love and consolation of the parties. Obviously, people marry for emotional as well as rational reasons.

How does a Church annulment differ from a civil annulment or a civil divorce?

A civil annulment, like a Church annulment, is a declaration that the marriage contract was invalid from the beginning. For instance, if a young woman was under the legal age of consent, the marriage is *ipso facto* invalid. Civil annulments free both parties from all obligations pertaining to alimony and property rights. Church annulments have no civil effects regarding property rights. This is why the Church actually asks the couple to settle the civil effects of the breakup by getting a divorce first.

A civil divorce is a legal dissolution of the marriage contract. In a divorce, the bond that once existed is legally severed by the state. The Catholic Church does not believe in divorce. It can never sever a true marriage bond.

A Church annulment is not the severing of an existing marriage bond. It merely says there never was a valid bond in the first place. Therefore the marriage contract was never legally binding.

Before the annulment process begins, the Church must be sure that reconciliation is no longer possible. This is necessary to protect the Church. In the past there were cases where a spouse opposed to the breakup of the marriage sued the Catholic Church for the "alienation of affections."

Would it be grounds for an annulment if the person you married was not baptized?

No. Before the marriage between a baptized and an unbaptized person takes place, a dispensation from disparity of cult is required. If the marriage took place without this dispensation, it could be annulled.

In special circumstances, the Church can grant a Privilege of the Faith, which is the dissolution of a valid but non-sacramental marriage.

The privilege comes in two models: The first is called the "Pauline Privilege" and is based on Paul's First Epistle to the Corinthians (1 Cor 7). If a marriage between two non-baptized parties breaks up, and one of them converts to Christianity, the convert may be permitted to enter into a new marriage with a Catholic by permission of the local bishop. St. Paul allowed this because so many marriages were breaking up in the early Church community.

The second type is called the "Petrine Privilege." This involves a marriage between a baptized person and a non-baptized person. Consult with a canon lawyer to see if you are eligible for such a privilege.

Would it be grounds for an annulment if the person you married refused to help you raise the children in the Catholic faith?

No. The partners have to work these difficulties out beforehand. The non-Catholic party is no longer asked to make promises to raise the children Catholic, but the Catholic party is asked to take every reasonable measure to see to the Catholic upbringing of the children. The validity of the marriage does not hinge on this issue. If, however, other circumstances existed, e.g., a husband refused to help raise the children in a general sense—no money, no emotional support, no real parental presence—this could be grounds for an annulment on the basis of a failure to live up to one's solemn promises. The grounds might be labeled "a lack of due discretion," which means, "Had I known this guy would turn out to be such an obstacle to a normal life, I never would have married him." A lack of knowledge about the deepest character traits of a person can be grounds for an annulment.

What happens to the children if an annulment is granted? Are they regarded as illegitimate?

No. As mentioned above, this is a common misconception. *The legitimacy of children is not affected by the annulment.* In the eyes of the Church, the children are considered the legitimate offspring of a union that failed. As a matter of canon law, the marriage was declared to be legally invalid. The children are legitimate in every respect. An illegitimate child is a child who is born out of wedlock. If the parents were married at the time their children were born, they are legitimate children.

Who can request a Church annulment?

Catholics and non-Catholics who are married in the Church have the right to petition the Marriage Tribunal to examine the validity of their marriage bond. Either spouse may initiate the case. The person who opens the case is called the petitioner. The other party is called the respondent.

Are the marriages of all non-Catholics presumed to be valid?

Yes. To annul such a marriage on canonical grounds, the non-Catholic would have to petition a competent tribunal which is either in the diocese where he or she lives or the one where the marriage took place.

Who would I contact first about obtaining an annulment?

In most dioceses you would start with your parish priest. He can provide you with the guidelines for beginning the process in the diocesan tribunal. If for some reason you find it necessary to side-step the local priest, call the diocesan tribunal or the chancery office and explain your problem.

Would the average parish priest have enough experience to help a couple submit their case in the best way possible? Or should the petitioner seek out a priest who is well informed about canon law?

The more experienced the priest the better. If your parish priest is unfamiliar with the annulment process, he will probably advise you to go to someone on the tribunal staff. Beware of any priest who simply gives you a form to complete. Find someone with experience before you submit your petition to the tribunal. The exact wording is very important. You may gloss over something crucial. For instance, if there is anything at all which touches on psychological problems, be sure to mention it.

If the case is complicated, you should seek the advice of a canon lawyer or someone with specialized training in these matters. Some parishes have people who went through the annulment process themselves. They can answer a lot of your questions. Anyone who is knowledgeable about the tribunal process can be of help. Most tribunals will supply an advocate to help you once they accept the case.

What are some of the steps you have to go through to obtain an annulment?

You will have to write a brief history of the marriage. The tribunal wants information about your family background, the courtship, the wedding, the honeymoon, the early days of your marriage, how your relationship developed, and how it eventually failed. This information is important because the tribunal must determine whether the marriage vows were validly exchanged. *The purpose is*

not to blame anyone, but to examine the circumstances leading up to the marriage and to study the reasons why it
ended in divorce.

Raking up the past is very difficult for most people
because it brings back painful memories. Don't be dis-
couraged. *The process can be an important catharsis that will
help you.* Tell as much as you can about how your dreams
were shattered and why you had to call it quits. If you
have trouble writing such things, try telling your story to
a friend with a tape recorder running. Then transcribe and
edit it so that it will read well.

Most people admit that even though this process opens
old wounds, there is something very healing about releas-
ing the pain that has been trapped inside. You may even
begin to see things about yourself or your spouse that you
never saw before. One woman told me she actually came
to a peaceful sense of closure after she wrote the story of
her failed marriage.

After you submit your marital history, the tribunal will
let you know whether or not you have sufficient grounds
for an annulment. If the tribunal agrees to hear your case,
they will assign a staff member as your advocate to guide
you through the rest of the process.

The tribunal will request the name and address of your
former spouse. You will also be asked to provide the
names of parents, friends, neighbors or anyone who knew
you before and during the marriage. At least two good
witnesses should be named in order to support the truth-
fulness of your statements. All this testimony is held in
the strictest confidence.

Why does the ex-spouse have to be contacted?

It's only fair that your spouse knows you are seeking an annulment. *Both spouses have a right to offer their testimony to the tribunal.* There is no need to have any personal contact with your former spouse. The testimony is taken separately. If an ex-spouse cannot be located or refuses to cooperate, the case can still proceed on the basis of the other evidence. In special circumstances where the malice of a respondent might put you in danger, the tribunal will take care to protect you from any contact. Don't be afraid to tell your whole story to the tribunal officials.

What if the tribunal refuses to accept your case?

If the tribunal says you do not have canonical grounds for an annulment, it means they will not hear the case. Everyone is entitled to submit a case, but no one has an absolute right to a formal hearing. If the tribunal refuses to accept your case because of insufficient grounds, it may be possible that you haven't submitted enough information. In that case, ask the tribunal for another canon lawyer. Get a second opinion. Perhaps you can resubmit your case using different grounds.

Why does the tribunal need witnesses?

The purpose of the witnesses is to support and verify the petitioner's testimony. Friends and family members can also serve as character witnesses by testifying to your honesty and integrity. Your credibility as a petitioner is very important.

Are the procedures in these cases similar to the procedures in a civil court?

Yes, similar but not identical. The Marriage Tribunal operates according to a set of procedures that are strictly enumerated in the *Code of Canon Law. Church cases are not decided by jury, but by a panel of three judges.* There is also a Defender of the Bond, who tries to protect the permanence of the marriage bond, and a Procurator Advocate, who argues in favor of the petitioner.

Three judges study the case and render a decision based on the evidence. If the judges turn in a split decision with two judges in favor of the annulment, and one judge against, the majority vote wins. This becomes an affirmative decision in the court of first instance. An annulment is not granted until there are two concurring affirmative judgments from two different tribunals. If you receive an affirmative judgment from the first court, your case goes to a court of second instance, usually in a different diocese, where three new judges decide to uphold or reject the opinion of the first court.

An affirmative decision in the court of second instance results in an annulment. If the second court does not approve the decision of the first court, you can appeal the case to the Roman Rota. The Rota is the court of third instance. It deals with the most difficult cases.

Who actually has to appear before the tribunal?

It depends on the case. In Defect of Form cases, no one has to appear. These are cases involving Catholics who married before a justice of the peace or a minister of another faith. Such cases require only an administrative process, with no need for testimony or witnesses. All you have to do is prove that you are a baptized Catholic who married outside of the Church. Have your pastor send in a recent copy of your baptismal certificate, your marriage certificate and your civil divorce decree. Within a few weeks, you will receive a decree of nullity.

A formal annulment case is more complicated and time consuming. Let's suppose, for instance, that a man is seeking an annulment on the grounds that his wife never intended to have children. He has the task of proving his wife's intent prior to the marriage. Witnesses may be found who will testify that the woman was obsessed with her figure, or that she always kept little children at a distance, or that they heard her say that she never wanted to have a child and took birth control pills or used some other form of contraception without her husband's knowledge. This would be evidence. However, unless someone actually heard her say, prior to marriage, that she was never going to have children, it is difficult to prove her intention at the time of the marriage. If two witnesses support the husband's testimony, the case becomes more solid.

If the wife admits that she never had any intention of having children, the case is strengthened by this confession. If, however, the wife accuses the husband of lying, and says she always wanted children, and only practiced birth control from time to time, her husband would have a real problem. Who should the tribunal believe?

The whole idea of a formal hearing is to get to the truth. Lies are usually uncovered. That's why it's always better to tell the truth when you give testimony.

I remember a bizarre case where a husband claimed that his former wife was really a man. He said it was an arranged marriage, and he went to another country to claim his bride. On their wedding night, he discovered that she was a female impersonator, who married to acquire U.S. citizenship. It was quite a story, but was it true? The tribunal contacted the ex-spouse to verify the claim. It turned out to be entirely bogus. She was a full blooded female, who had remarried and given birth to two children. The petitioner was a preposterous liar, who thought that no one would check his story. His case was, of course, rejected.

How much does an annulment cost?

No one is denied the right to apply for and obtain an annulment because they are poor. The cost varies slightly from diocese to diocese, but the average cost at this writing is between $500 and $1,000. The cost depends on the size of the diocese and the corresponding size of the tribunal office staff.

Why does the Church charge anything for annulments?

The fees help defray the cost of salaries, the education of canon lawyers, the office upkeep, postage and the other expenses involved in the annulment process. In most cases, the fee does not cover the actual costs involved. Nearly every diocesan tribunal operates in the red. In the past fifteen years, the Church tribunals in the United States have collectively been more than $15 million dollars in the red annually. This is not a money-making operation.

Does it help your case if you know someone important in the Church?

No. If you try to pull strings it will probably work against you. I directed a marriage tribunal for ten years, and the bishop never once asked me to advance the process for someone special. Power or influence should make no difference in whether or not an annulment is granted. Think about it. You cannot bribe six different judges in two different dioceses.

Sometimes a pastor might ask where the case stands, hoping to find out how much longer the process will take. That is a reasonable inquiry, and we try to give an estimate, but we can't make any promises. That is why it is never a good idea to set the date for a new marriage before you have the annulment in hand. Those who do, end up trying to put pressure on the tribunal to grant the annulment. Such a strategy is counter-productive.

How long does the process usually take?

The length of the process will depend on the complexity of the case, the local caseload and the difficulties encountered in obtaining evidence. *Most cases take about a year. Church law states that the process should be completed within 18 months.*

What if an annulment is not granted?

Remember, you have to prove your case. Annulments are denied if you lack sufficient evidence to overthrow the presumption of validity. If you are denied an annulment, you may feel free to contact the tribunal staff for an explanation.

If you are denied a Church annulment, can you reintroduce the case?

Yes, you can either appeal the decision to Rome, or submit new evidence to have the case retried on new grounds. You won't get very far if you present exactly the same case.

Can you go to a different diocese to reintroduce the case?

You can bring your case before the tribunal in the diocese where you live or where you have a quasi-domicile, like a summer home. You may also file your case in the diocese where the marriage took place. You may not randomly select any diocesan tribunal unless you have established a residence there.

Why was it so difficult in the past to obtain a Church annulment?

In past decades, many who were deserving of a marriage annulment were unable to obtain one for reasons that are all too human. Sometimes the parish priest was at fault, advising that there was no case when in fact there was. At other times, the tribunal's heavy caseload was the culprit. Due to understaffing, some cases just died on the vine and were abandoned. Occasionally, a case based on solid grounds remained stalled because a key witness refused to cooperate.

There is also the problem with human fallibility on the part of the judges. In the past, some judges have denied annulments because of an overly strict notion of the moral certitude required of them. Technically, a tribunal judge does not have to attain absolute certainty, which means that he has no fear of error. A judge may vote to grant the annulment based on a strong preponderance of evidence, while realizing that there is a possibility that he may be wrong. It is almost impossible to be free of all doubts in most cases. In a sense, the judges are exercising their conscience in rendering their decision, which is why they sometimes differ. Judging a marriage case is not an exact science.

Some petitions may be too difficult to prove with absolute certainty. For example, suppose a woman abhors the thought of sexual contact, and this only came to light after the marriage. Could this be considered fraud going to the heart of the marriage contract? Possibly, but more than likely there are psychological problems involved. Proving them is quite another matter. Suppose the couple breaks up, and she refuses to cooperate in an annulment process. How can a tribunal know if the husband is telling the truth? Proof that his wife always felt repulsed at the idea of sexual intercourse is not easy to produce. All we have is the husband's word. Is he telling the truth?

What about non-consummation cases?

The Church can and does dissolve non-consummated marriages. Cases where the marriage was never ratified by an act of sexual intercourse are rare, but they do exist. The Church teaches that a valid, consummated marriage cannot be dissolved by any civil or ecclesiastical authority. Consummation ratifies the consent. If the marriage was never consummated, the Church can formally dissolve the bond. Only the pope can grant dissolutions based on non-consummation.

One party is usually the cause of the problem, and that person would not be allowed to marry again in the Church unless the psychological or physical obstacle was corrected.

Have there been new developments in the efficiency of the tribunals?

Yes. Before 1960 very few formal cases were granted. Tribunal efficiency was at a low level. Only the strongest cases seemed to make it through, and most tribunals handled only a few formal cases a year.

Today, Church tribunals have become more efficient. The effort to deal with human needs in a pastoral way required a new approach. As far back as May of 1968, a special committee of the U.S. Canon Law Society began to review the effectiveness of the procedural laws. They developed a set of 27 norms for reforming the system, and these were accepted at the annual convention of the Canon Law Society in September 1968. These recommendations were then sent to the American bishops who approved them in their April 1969 meeting. After making a few changes, the bishops voted to forward the 27 suggested reforms to the Holy See for approval.

Rome gave permission for 23 of the 27 norms to be adopted in July of 1970. This was an experimental concession given to the Church in the United States. Some of these reforms were eventually put into the 1983 revision of the *Code of Canon Law.*

Are there any major developments regarding new grounds for an annulment?

The development of new knowledge in the fields of psychiatry, sociology and human behavior gave canon lawyers new insights into the nature of consent. For instance, we didn't know that certain psychological disorders affected a person's consent retroactively. A person may have appeared to be normal on the wedding day, but if we later learn that he or she was a paranoid schizophrenic, it would be like a time bomb waiting to explode. In the distant past, to get an annulment on psychological grounds, the petitioner had to produce psychological evaluations that proved a history of mental illness which predated the wedding ceremony. Today a psychiatric evaluation of a psychotic condition will often suffice, even if no prior diagnosis was available.

It may surprise you to know that much of the progress in our jurisprudence came from the Roman Rota. Decisions coming from these judges opened our eyes to new possibilities in the area of psychological capacity. If Rome allowed something, we knew that we were free to use the same arguments.

Could you give an example of the kind of Rotal decision that may have advanced the jurisprudence?

Yes. In a case recorded in the *Monitor Ecclesiasticus*, Volume Two, for 1968, the Roman Rota granted an annulment on the basis of immaturity. The judge stated that matrimonial consent cannot be validly given unless the contracting parties know that marriage is a permanent union between man and woman for the procreation of children. Father Mark Said, the judge in this case, raised the question: *Exactly what kind of knowledge is required?* He suggested that the required degree of knowledge must be appreciative knowledge, not merely conceptual knowledge. In other words, the person "must have sufficient discretion and maturity of judgment in order to give deliberate matrimonial consent." The "lack of due discretion" had always been grounds for annulment, but Fr. Said expanded that category to include cases of extreme immaturity. Up until then, we had never used the word "immaturity" to justify an annulment.

It was a breakthrough. Today, more cases are being heard on the grounds of "a lack of due discretion," than any other grounds. Of course, immaturity refers to a variety of flaws in the personality. We should not trivialize the grounds for nullity, but some people lack the necessary maturity of judgment to enter into and sustain the burdens and obligations of marriage. When this happens, there is probably an invalid consent.

Isn't it true that many young people today write their own version of their vows? Some say, "I will marry you for as long as I'm happy with you." They don't appreciate the permanent nature of marriage. Is it possible that many of these marriages might be canonically invalid?

The presumption of validity applies in every Catholic wedding, but the question you raise is a good one. Sometimes this presumption is wrong. No one is permitted to rewrite the vows in such a way as to privatize the marriage contract. Marriage is a permanent, exclusive union which is open to procreation. These essentials must be acknowledged in the exchange of vows.

What role does character play in all this?

In 1972, a Canadian theologian named Father Germain Lesage, OMI, writing in *Studia Canonica*, proposed 15 elements which he considered essential to true conjugal love. According to Lesage, if any one of these elements were lacking to a vital degree at the time the marriage was contracted, then the marriage would not be canonically valid. Over the years many judges have used Fr. Lesage's criteria in their decisions.

Can you name a few of these elements?

According to Lesage, to be a valid marriage, the union must have "oblatory love." This love is not aimed at one's own ego satisfaction, but instead provides for the welfare and happiness of the partner. There must also be "respect for conjugal morality, and for the partner's conscience in sexual relations."

Another element is "the respective responsibility of both the husband and wife in providing for the material welfare of the home, stability in work, and budgetary foresight." A man who refuses to go to work can create an intolerable situation for his wife and children who depend on him.

How does immaturity in relation to money matters become a factor?

We run into cases where the men have no interest in providing for the material well-being of their families. The wife is continually plagued with financial hardships. Sometimes these men work, but they do not bring home any money because of a gambling or an alcohol problem.

In the past many tribunals would not consider such cases for an annulment. Today, judges are more enlightened. Husbands who lack the will to take responsibility for the welfare of their families from the beginning exhibit an incapacitating defect. The validity of such a marriage is doubtful.

Can you give another example of a lack of conjugal love?

One thing considered necessary for true consent is the mastery of irrational passions, impulses or instincts. Chronic adulterers are suspect. Someone who is psychologically incapable of marital fidelity will not only cause the spouse constant humiliation, but will destroy all trust in the marriage. Exposing the innocent spouse to venereal diseases and even AIDS is gravely irresponsible. This is more than a question of occasional human weakness. When a person is a chronic violator of marital fidelity, it points to a psychological flaw which undermined the person's capacity to give true consent from the start of the marriage.

How do you determine if there is a real psychological disorder present?

The testimony of a psychiatrist or a psychologist helps. However, we do not always need a professional evaluation to ascertain whether the person had the capacity to sustain the burdens and obligations of marriage. When there is an obvious pattern of abuse, or a personality disorder, serious doubts might arise about the validity of the marriage.

If you make the determination that a person was not capable of entering into a valid marriage, aren't you also saying that he or she should never be allowed to marry in the future?

Yes and no. We believe growth is possible. We usually put a warning on the decision, requiring the culpable party to go for help. This warning on the annulment document alerts all priests that there is danger in allowing this person to enter into a new marriage. If the condition hasn't been corrected through counseling or psychological treatment, no new marriage in the Church will be permitted.

Is it true that the Church never used to give annulments for homosexuality?

Yes. Only in more recent times have annulments been granted on these grounds. When tribunals began putting the emphasis on the capacity of each individual to sustain the burdens of marriage, things changed. This was a shift in the emphasis from the efficient cause of the marriage, i.e., the act of consent, to the material cause, i.e., the capacity of the consenting party.

What do you mean?

This is a little complicated to explain. Marriage is traditionally viewed under two aspects: marriage *in fieri* (in the act of becoming), and marriage in *facto esse* (in what it actually is). The first stresses the quality of consent. Was it defective or not? The second is concerned with the individual's capacity to marry.

Marriage *in fieri* considers the man and the woman as consenting subjects, and therefore, as the efficient cause of the contract. Traditionally, the main emphasis for attacking the validity of a marriage has been on the quality of the consent given on the day of the wedding. The tribunal asks: Did they mean what they said? Did they intend to enter a permanent, exclusive union? Various forms of defective consent constituted the grounds on which most annulments were granted in those days. If a person never intended to have children, the consent was defective, and the presumption of validity was overturned.

Marriage, when viewed *in facto esse,* looks at the material cause of the sacrament. Here validity depends on the fitness of the two parties to enter into and sustain the burdens and obligations of marriage. If one party lacks the capacity to accept or fulfill the obligations of married life, there can be no true union.

It is the mutual exchange of the love commitment that constitutes the matter and form of the sacrament. A homosexual does not have the capacity to make a lifelong commitment in a heterosexual union. The contract, in most cases, does not become effective because a Catholic marriage presupposes that both parties are heterosexual.

In other words, the homosexual is really not suited for a heterosexual marriage?

Correct. However, there are degrees of bisexuality that are quite mysterious. Not every marriage is *ipso facto* invalid because of homosexual acts committed by one party.

In the past the Church refused to touch these cases because homosexuality was regarded as a sin to be over-come rather then a sexual orientation or state of life. True homosexuality renders a person incapable of entering a true heterosexual marriage. There's a difference, however, between bad faith and incapacity. A person in bad faith knowingly uses the marriage as a cover. Sometimes the homosexual is in denial and he or she marries in good faith. In time, the condition becomes painfully obvious, but the couple still wants the marriage and they struggle to maintain it. Such marriages are not *ipso facto* invalid. In fact, they are as blessed as any sacramental marriage. We never rule out God's grace in difficult situations.

How would you answer the criticism that too many annulments are being granted today? It sometimes appears that if you dig hard enough you can always find some basis for the nullity of a marriage.

There are millions of divorces each year, but only a few thousand annulments. We are only touching the surface. The Apostolic Signatura is the Church's highest authority in judicial matters, and they are constantly on guard. If the Holy See becomes suspicious about a problem in some marriage tribunal, they act swiftly.

The judge's only concern is that he render justice. Expanding the grounds for annulments and simplifying the procedures have proven to be a good thing. All of these reforms had the approval of the Holy See every step of the way.

Right now I think we are doing the best we can with what we have. I respect the men and women who staff our tribunals. They work hard in difficult circumstances and they deserve our trust.

The reason more Church annulments are being granted today than in the past is not because of laxity, but because of a better understanding of the nature of marriage. Years ago, tribunals were too narrow and too uninformed about the psychological condition of the petitioners and respondents. We know more now. The issue is one of justice. It is not a matter of giving everyone what they want; it is a matter of giving everyone their due, no more, no less.

Many dedicated priests and lay people are working in our tribunals, but it is still an imperfect human system. Sometimes witnesses lie and annulments are granted in error. Sometimes judges miss something important and tilt their judgment incorrectly. Mistakes happen, but for the most part, such mistakes are rare.

Because the tribunal is such a human system, the conscience of an individual must be respected, as I will explain more fully in chapter 4.

What do you think is the central issue in running a good tribunal?

Fidelity to the truth is always the central issue. The bishop's role in caring for his flock requires that he provides adequate pastoral care for the people of his diocese. That includes all men and women who have suffered the tragedy of a broken marriage.

There is much more to pastoral care than merely setting up a tribunal. The bishop must ask himself: What kind of a tribunal am I running? Is it too legalistic? Is the judicial vicar more interested in protocol and canonical exactitude than in finding the truth and helping the brokenhearted people who come before him? Is his Vicar a pastorally oriented jurist or merely a canonical robot?

The Second Vatican Council taught in *The Constitution of the Church*, Section 27 that, "Bishops govern the particular Churches entrusted to them as the vicars and ambassadors of Christ . . . This power, which they personally exercise in Christ's name, is proper, ordinary and immediate, although its exercise is ultimately regulated by the supreme authority of the Church and can be circumscribed by certain limits for the advantage of the Church. . . . In virtue of this power, bishops have the sacred right and the duty before the Lord to make laws for their subjects, to pass judgment on them, and to moderate everything pertaining to the ordering of worship and the apostolate."

This teaching gives the bishop quite a bit of discretionary power.

The three German bishops mentioned in the first chapter (cf. p. 16) were no doubt trying to fulfill this mandate. They were corrected by the Holy See, but at least they were trying to deal with a serious pastoral problem. They realized that a legalistic approach to these cases was not working. The presumption of validity in many cases works harshly against the innocent victims of deceit and fraud. Some tribunals are inadequately staffed for the caseloads they handle. New remedies are needed, and the bishop must get involved.

Back in 1969, 57 out of the 153 U.S. tribunals in existence at the time did not even render one formal decision a year; 23 more published only one decision; and 9 gave only two decisions in that same year. Fortunately this situation has changed for the better, but there are still overwhelming caseloads in most dioceses. Staffing is limited, and priests are in short supply. More lay people are being trained for tribunal work and this is good.

The bishop can show concern for his people by seeing to it that there is a professional approach taken in the tribunal. That does not mean a legalistic, officious or uncaring approach. Professionalism simply calls for efficient, courteous service and a devotion to justice tempered with mercy.

Do some people fall through the cracks because of legalism?

Times are changing, but God's law is unchanging. Some officials make God's law appear narrower and more severe than it really is. If the supreme law is charity, then charity as well as objectivity must pervade the interpretation of law. Justice tempered with mercy is the very meaning of canonical equality. This amounts to a judicious application of the general law to a particular human situation.

In a legal system where many tribunals put human lives on hold for years while a half-hearted investigation takes place, the Church is in no position to criticize those who walk away and follow their conscience. Some people may be subjectively deluded about their right to an annulment, but others have asked the Church for bread and have been handed a stone. When a person gets the silent treatment, or is treated rudely, there is no excuse.

Some people are too fragile emotionally to go through an annulment process. I've also known of cases where the petitioner had grounds for an annulment, but did not want to hurt the other party or the children by exposing their hidden secrets or by opening old wounds. Those who feel they cannot go through the legal process should not be forced to file for an annulment.

The law is designed to serve the common good, but at the same time, the mission of Christ is to save individuals. We must find the balance. In the words of Ivo of Chartres (c. 1040-1116 A.D.): "We urge the prudent reader, when judging the merits of contrary texts, to keep before his eyes the end of law, which is the salvation of souls, and the fact that some things are said in a spirit of moderation and mercy."

When I first started working in the marriage tribunal, the system of justice was uneven at best, and downright slipshod at worst. In an article I wrote for *Commonweal* magazine in 1965, I argued that there are times when the laity can and should exercise their conscience and trust themselves to the mercy of God. So many marriages are disasters from day one that it seems inconceivable to me that God would bind someone for life to an abusive person.

Some people simply follow their consciences and entrust the matter to God's mercy. Those who believe that their first marriage was never valid and have no sense of sin regarding their second marriage are in good faith. Their problem is that the Church does not recognize the second marriage.

If for some reason the annulment process fails to remedy the situation, the internal forum solution may come into play.

In the next chapter we will examine the concept of conscience and the internal forum.

CHAPTER 4

What is the Internal Forum?

WHILE the principle of indissolubility is never in doubt, the binding nature of a particular marriage can be in doubt. The role of conscience is sometimes involved in resolving these doubts.

The internal forum is your conscience. The external forum is the Church's entire administrative and judicial system. *The Pastoral Constitution on the Church in the Modern World,* a document of the Second Vatican Council, defined conscience as "the most secret core and sanctuary of the person. There one is alone with God, there one's innermost self perceives God's voice" (#16).

It has always been part of the teaching of the Church that the individual conscience is the proximate norm of morality, while the law is a remote norm. You are always obliged to follow the dictates of your conscience, even if your conscience is in disagreement with legitimate authority. Following your conscience is not merely a right, but a duty. If a conflict arises between your conscience and Church law, you are obliged to pursue the matter, and seek further enlightenment.

For example, what happens to a person who wakes up from the nightmare of a disastrous first marriage, obtains a divorce, and later finds healing love in a new relationship? That person might believe deeply that God sent the new love as a special gift, but the Church seems to be saying, "No. You are living in sin." Only God knows the state of a person's soul. The Church is saying that the first marriage is presumed to be valid.

Who is right?

The question a divorced person must ask is this: Was my marriage a *true* Christian marriage? It is the same question the ecclesiastical court asks. An annulment will be given or denied on the basis of the court's finding.

The tribunal operates in the *external forum.* The judges must rely on evidence, witnesses and testimony. Judges sometimes falter in finding the truth because witnesses lie and human error is a fact of life. It is also very difficult to prove that one person had a defective intention during or prior to the actual marriage ceremony.

The internal forum is a pastoral remedy which relies on conscience, usually in the privacy of the confessional. It is not an expression of subjectivism gone wild. It is not the privatization of religion. The term *internal forum* in this context refers to the exercise of an informed conscience.

There are Church publications that guide priests in their task of applying the laws of the Church to personal situations. For example, in the *Code of Canon Law* the following principles are used (cf. *The Code of Canon Law: Text and Commentary*, Paulist Press, p. 6).

1. The principle and essential object of canon law is to determine and safeguard the rights and obligations of each individual person with

respect to the rights and obligations of others and of the whole community.

2. The Code should improve harmony between the external forum and the internal forum, reducing conflict between them to a minimum, especially in regard to the sacraments . . .

These two principles help us to interpret the universal laws of the Church and apply them properly to concrete pastoral situations. Since the Church is dealing with an individual's natural law right to marry, it must be very careful to be fair. Canon law governs the external forum with respect to what is required for the common good. The internal forum pertains to the forum of conscience.

The American hierarchy petitioned the Holy See for a ruling on the internal forum back in the 1970s. This confidential paper entitled "The Pastoral Care of Divorced and Remarried Catholics" established the fundamental points of doctrine stressing the holiness, the sacramentality and the indissolubility of Christian marriage. Then it discussed the spiritual ministry to divorced Catholics, including the pastoral use of the internal forum. It was an attempt to be more pastoral than legalistic. The Holy See never replied.

This probably means that the internal forum is left for us to discern. Since parish priests are the ones who administer the sacraments and hear confessions, it is they who can offer the greatest help to their parishioners. They know that an informed conscience must be obeyed, and they have the task of training their people to inform their consciences in the light of God's law. At the same time they must guard against abuse.

The meaning of conscience is clarified by paragraph #16 from Vatican II's *Pastoral Constitution on the Church in the Modern World, "Gaudium et Spes"* (Joy and Hope): "In the depths of their conscience human beings detect a law which they do not make for themselves but which they must obey. Its voice always summons them to love and to do what is good and to shun what is evil. At the right moment it resounds in the secrecy of the heart: 'do this, avoid that.' The dignity of the human person lies in obeying it; and according to this law one will be judged (cf. Rom 2:14-16)."

In other words, we will be judged on our obedience to the voice of conscience. Human dignity requires us to act through conscience, motivated from within, and not through blind impulse or merely external pressure. There are times when your conscience will challenge you to have the courage of your convictions.

John Cardinal Newman in his *Grammar of Assent* speaks of conscience as "our great internal teacher of religion." He insisted, however, that conscience is not a license to take up any or no religion. On the contrary, it is a stern monitor: "Conscience has rights because it has duties." Conscience binds one to the law of God. It attests to a higher intelligence.

What happens if a person in a second marriage believes his or her first marriage was never a true marriage? The bishops of Holland had something to say about matters involving a conflict between a just law and personal conscience: "In such cases, a thorough discussion with a prudent spiritual director can free a person from much unnecessary fear. It can even happen that a believer comes to the conclusion that his marriage does not bind him in conscience." This quote was taken from the Dutch Catechism, written nearly 50 years ago.

The *Catechism of the Catholic Church* published in 1994, quotes St. Augustine, "Return to your conscience, question it. . . . Turn inward brethren, and in everything you do see God as your witness." It continues:

> "Man has the right to act in conscience and in freedom . . . he must not be forced to act contrary to his conscience."
>
> "Conscience must be informed and moral judgment enlightened. A well-formed conscience is upright and truthful."

Morality is not a matter of locality and private opinion. There is such a thing as objective evil. The Ten Commandments were not ten suggestions. "Thou shalt not commit adultery" is a serious warning. Infidelity is a sin, and the Church must teach and defend the divine law. Conscience is an internal compass which guides us in our moral decisions. However, before a law is morally binding, your conscience must understand and accept the law as applying to the case at hand. No one is bound to obey something that he or she does not believe is binding. No one can be asked to do something that is morally impossible for them.

When two people marry in the Church before qualified witnesses, the marriage is presumed to be valid. Suppose, however, that the groom had a lover on the side and had no intention of giving her up. On the wedding day, he vowed that he was entering an exclusive relationship, but he was lying. He was lying to God, to his bride and to himself. This marriage was invalid because the husband perpetrated a fraud going to the heart of the marriage contract. Nevertheless, the marriage is presumed to be valid until such time as the contrary is proven in an ecclesiastical court of law. It is a legal presumption that works against the facts of the case.

Suppose the wife finds out two years later that he had been unfaithful to her from the beginning. She leaves him, gets a civil divorce and seeks an annulment. The husband refuses to cooperate, and like the true liar that he is, denies that he was ever unfaithful. She has no solid proof, no photographs, no eye witnesses and no confession from her husband. However, she knows deep in her heart that he is guilty. The look on his face when he returned home late at night with no explanation, the withdrawal of affection and his lies—all pointed in one direction. Unfortunately her suspicions do not constitute sufficient evidence to prove her case to the satisfaction of the marriage tribunal. She *does* have a case, but she lacks the evidence required by the tribunal to prove it.

Can she marry again in a civil ceremony without committing a sin? Yes, if her conscience is clear and there is no malice in her heart.

If she knows that her husband defrauded her, she can and must follow her conscience. She is not truly married to the man who lied to her. She married her first husband in good faith, but he deceived her. Since it was not a true marriage, her natural law right to marry is still intact.

In the external forum, the Church still presumes that her first marriage is binding, but in the internal forum of conscience, she knows that she is not bound to her first husband. She also believes deeply that God will bless her second marriage, and she is right. God is just, but in some cases, the tribunal system, following a legal presumption, is not. Being legally correct does not guarantee true justice.

The internal forum solution occasionally serves as a safety valve for the inadequacies of our tribunals. They deal with massive caseloads involving complex allegations that are not always possible to prove. In the United States, thousands of deserving couples have come back to the sacraments through the internal forum, even though their present marriage was never technically revalidated in the Church. This solution is less than ideal, but it is necessary when the external forum fails to deliver justice.

In the past, Catholics were led to believe that the rewards of heaven or the pains of hell were directly related to the judgment of a few canon lawyers, but this is a truncated understanding of revelation. Jesus opposed the legalistic approach to human life with all his strength; he resisted it even to the point of death.

One's destiny before God is not necessarily based on one's juridical standing in the Catholic Church. Very few American Catholics under the age of 40 suffer from scruples in these matters, but countless others were formed differently, and they suffer severe emotional pain.

Those who have used the internal forum solution often long for the day when their state of life will be entirely vindicated by the Church. They look to the official Church for an open and honest remedy to their marital situation. They want an annulment, but can't get one at this time.

In a perfect world, the tribunal would look at the petitioner and say, "We see you are telling the truth. Your husband never intended an exclusive relationship. Therefore, you are still free to marry, and here is your annulment."

Suppose the husband denies his infidelity and offers counter-charges. Confusion about the facts arises. The judges may want more evidence. So if the tribunal in this case says, "Sorry, you don't have a strong enough case," that doesn't necessarily mean God is saying, "You are validly marred to number one, and you are living in sin."

If your first marriage is not valid before God, your natural law right to marry remains intact. Consequently, if you marry again, this time before a justice of the peace, it can be argued that your second marriage is not sinful, provided of course that your second spouse was also free to marry. Marriage is a natural law right, and the natural law supersedes ecclesiastical law.

Could you be more specific about the internal forum? How does one exercise one's conscience in these matters?

It may help if we look at another scenario. Suppose a young woman was abandoned by her husband within a year of their marriage. He told her that he only married her to give their baby a name, and he never intended to stay with her permanently. However, before they were married, he signed a sworn document stating that he intended a permanent union. The Church cannot be faulted for holding people to their word. In so serious a matter as matrimony, a signed document is not dismissed lightly. The tribunal judges could speculate that he might at first have intended to marry for life, but later changed his mind, in which case the marriage contract was valid. The wife would need two or more witnesses to establish conclusively that her husband never intended to stay in the marriage, and that his signed promise of marrying for life was a lie.

Where does this young woman stand? Her husband has deceived her, but unless he confesses or she finds corroborative evidence to convince the Church court of the invalidity of her marriage, the presumption of validity stands. If he disappears and no one comes forward to support her testimony, she would be out of luck as far as a formal annulment is concerned.

Today, most tribunals would accept her testimony as true and base the case on her honesty, showing her to be a person who would not lie in a matter this serious. Of course all the circumstances of the case support her testimony. If the tribunal does not grant the annulment, she still has her conscience to guide her to do this. She must take into consideration the law and God's will as she understands it.

Now let's suppose she meets a good man who was never married before. They fall in love. She will need the courage of her convictions as she faces the frightening alternative of either living alone for the rest of her life, or marrying outside the Church. She wants to do the right thing, but at first she isn't sure what to do. She eventually decides to marry before a justice of the peace.

What happens to her Catholicity?

She is still a Catholic. Her second marriage, which is now presumed to be invalid by the official Church, becomes for her "a good conscience marriage." In her conscience, the new marriage is valid before God, even though it is technically invalid in the eyes of the Church.

In such a case, two serious questions arise:
1. Can the parties of this new marriage consider themselves to be true members of the Church? Yes.
2. May they receive the Eucharist without sinning? Let their conscience be their guide. A matter of this kind should be discussed in the privacy of the confessional.

According to the circumstances of the case as described above, the couple is not living in sin.

In his Exhortation, *Familiaris Consortio* (n. 84) Pope John Paul II made the point that "reconciliation in the sacrament of Penance, which would open the way to the Eucharist, can only be granted to those who repenting of having broken the sign of the covenant and fidelity to Christ, are sincerely ready to undertake a way of life that is in no way in contradiction to the indissolubility of marriage."

Since this woman is not living in sin, she is now living in a good conscience union. *The Catechism of the Catholic Church* (par. 1782) states: "Man has the right to act in conscience and in freedom."

Is she excommunicated for entering an invalid marriage?

No, she is not excommunicated. In these matters, the penalty of excommunication was *never* part of the universal law of the Church. Over 150 years ago, divorced American Catholics who remarried outside the Church were excommunicated. The American bishops introduced this penalty in the nineteenth century to discourage intermarriage of American Catholics with non-Catholics. This was never a universal law of the Church. *Today, no one is excommunicated because of an invalid marriage.* This penalty has been totally and retroactively removed.

What about the sacrament of Matrimony? Can the second marriage in this case be considered a sacrament?

Technically, no. However, a sacrament is a mysterious sign of Christ's presence.

We are made members of the Church through baptism. This gives us the right to receive all the other sacraments. The sacrament of Matrimony is conferred by the husband and wife in their mutual exchange of consent. It is not unreasonable to assume they are in a good faith sacramental marriage. Officially, of course, they have entered an invalid union.

What steps should one take in order to reach an internal forum solution?

When in doubt, go for help. Find a priest who will listen to your story in the privacy of the confessional. The priest can help you form a good conscience according to the circumstances of your case. This transfers the case from the external forum (the marriage tribunal), to the internal forum, the tribunal of mercy.

The priest cannot give permission to the couple to live together or to receive Holy Communion, but he can offer encouragement for them to follow their consciences. The priest merely reassures the parties that in a delicate matter such as this, they can trust their consciences. He may even instruct the parties that they are morally obliged to follow an informed conscience.

Ultimately, they must have the courage to act on what they know to be true in their heart of hearts.

How could the second marriage be valid if a priest did not marry them?

The word "valid" is a legal term. Technically, her second marriage would be "invalid" before the Church, but morally it would be "valid" before God. The Lord knows the real story. Jesus can bless the second marriage just as he can heal the pain of the past.

In such cases can the parties begin to receive Holy Communion right away?

They should receive the sacrament of Reconciliation first. If I were the confessor in this case, I would hear their confession, give them a penance, absolve them and then check with the local pastor for his approval on the Holy Communion issue. If he thought it might cause scandal, I would advise the couple to go to another parish.

When a person is inwardly well disposed and is not consciously living in sin, it is reasonable to assume that he or she may receive Holy Communion. Baptism gives you the right to exercise your conscience and to unite yourself with the Lord by the reception of his most sacred Body and Blood. We must not trivialize the sacrament of the Eucharist and make it available indiscriminately to one and all, but neither may we deny it to those who approach the altar sincerely and in good faith.

What do you mean by "scandal"?

True scandal is a form of outrage at someone's objectionable conduct; whereas, pharisaical scandal is a rash judgment, a way of unjustly judging people. Some people become upset when couples who are divorced and remarried outside the Church receive Holy Communion. They don't know all the facts. However, if there is a possibility of scandal, it might be better for the couple to attend Mass and receive Communion in a different parish. If the couple is virtually unknown in their own parish and there is little danger of scandal, most pastors would allow them to receive in the parish where they live.

What do these people tell their friends and relatives when all of a sudden they start receiving Communion again?

They should say it's a matter between themselves and God. If people persist, they should simply say, "I can't believe that you're asking such a personal question!"

Can a couple in an internal forum marriage ever publicly revalidate their marriage vows in Church?

If you're asking whether they can marry in the Church, the answer is no, not without a Church annulment. *A priest is not permitted to officiate at a marriage involving someone who has been previously married and who has not had that marriage annulled.* Since the marriage ceremony takes place in the external forum, an annulment would have to be obtained before a priest could validly perform the ceremony.

It would be wrong for a priest to simulate the sacrament. Any priest who does so would be in violation of the law. However, the couple may ask for a blessing. If a priest can bless animals, he can certainly bless people as long as he does not pretend to be marrying them officially.

This is a flawed solution I admit, but it is better than allowing them to feel utterly rejected by the very Church Jesus Christ established to save and comfort them.

Can a person who has gone through the internal forum solution get a letter of recommendation from a parish to be a godparent or a Confirmation sponsor?

If a pastor is convinced that this person would make a good godparent or sponsor, he may choose to exercise his conscience and write such a letter. We are interested in the truth in these matters. If I were the pastor and I knew all the circumstances about the marriage, and I knew the person was faithful in the practice of the faith, I would write the letter. If a letter is not required in advance, I would advise the person to just show up and sponsor the child without going into any detail.

Can people who have gone through the internal forum solution become a eucharistic minister or a lector?

Probably not, though some pastors have allowed it. I remember a case where a G.I. in the Second World War married a French girl in the Church. When he returned from battle to take her back to the States, she was gone. He found out later that she had married six other G.I.'s to collect the insurance money if they were killed. He could never prove his case to the satisfaction of the tribunal because in those years, the tribunals were much stricter. He eventually remarried outside the Church and for many years never dared to receive Holy Communion. I helped him ease his conscience and return to the sacraments.

No one in the parish knew about his French bride. If I were his pastor, I would have no hesitation in allowing him to be a eucharistic minister if he requested it. But I would also bombard the tribunal with character testimony to get him the annulment he deserves.

Suppose a "good conscience" couple gets a new pastor who does not approve of the internal forum. Can the new pastor rescind the couple's internal forum solution and deny them Communion or full participation in parish life?

No. A new pastor cannot rescind the conscience decision of another person. He might ask them not to receive Holy Communion in his parish. If that happened, I would advise the couple to accept the decision. You have to respect the pastor's conscience, if you expect him to respect yours. Go to the nearest parish where you feel comfortable. Better yet, try to reopen your annulment case in the tribunal.

If a never married woman marries a man who does not have an annulment is she allowed to receive Holy Communion?

Presuming that he was validly married in the Catholic Church, this new marriage would be considered to be invalid and she should not receive Communion. However, should she ever divorce him, she would not require an annulment to remarry in the Catholic Church.

What does the *Code of Canon Law* say about using your conscience when you are in serious conflict over some doctrinal Church teaching?

This quote from the 1983 *Code of Canon Law* has to do with conscience and the assent of faith required of us in matters of Church teaching: "The principles of the pursuit of truth and the primacy of conscience still come into play. In other words, dissent is possible . . . The search for truth is everyone's duty and right . . ."

The Code acknowledges the right to dissent from Church teaching if one's conscience demands it, but that doesn't make them right. The truth is not multiple. They may be subjectively convinced of an error, but that doesn't make them right.

Are there any examples where bishops have allowed people to follow their consciences in marital matters?

Yes, but you do not need anyone's permission to follow your conscience. You must follow your conscience with or without permission. In July 1968, when Pope Paul VI condemned artificial birth control in the encyclical *Humanae Vitae,* bishops all over the world were quick to respond. While stressing the *obligation of obedience,* they very clearly left the door open for *freedom of conscience.* Here are a few examples where the distinction between the authority issue and the moral issue is carefully stated. On the one hand loyalty to the pope is stressed, on the other, fidelity to one's conscience is conceded.

Belgium

On August 30, 1968, the Belgian bishops issued a statement which supports the authority of the encyclical, but includes the following paragraph:

"Someone, however, who is competent in the matter under consideration and capable of forming a personal and well-founded judgment—which necessarily presupposes a sufficient amount of knowledge—may, after a serious examination before God, come to other conclusions on certain points. In such a case he has the right to follow his conviction provided that he remains sincerely disposed to continue his inquiry."

Holland

About the same time, the bishops of Holland issued this statement:

"In this critical hour we realize that many Catholics are feeling uneasy. Many people feel disappointed by the papal encyclical, particularly by the declaration on contraceptives. These Catholics are being tested in their faith . . .

" . . . The consequences of the encyclical have worldwide meaning and only after a long time and deep thinking can one understand its scope. You will understand that your bishops will be able to offer the guidance you need only after serious consultation with theologians and other experts. This guidance will undoubtedly be offered to you; but probably it will take time. A Catholic owes respect to the word and authority of the Pope. The individual conscience cannot ignore such an authoritative declaration as this encyclical. For that matter, many factors that determine the individual conscience with regard to the conjugal act are already clear: for example, mutual love, relations in the family and social circumstances. We Catholics believe in papal infallibility. Though this encyclical is no infallible dogmatic declaration, it is still a true plea for the dignity of life and an appeal for responsibility in sexuality and marriage that is of very great importance in our society. May the discussion about this encyclical contribute to a more pure evaluation and functioning of authority inside the Church. Let us pray in these days for our Holy Father and for each other."

This statement is respectful of the pope, but mindful that the teaching has not been accepted by the individual conscience of many people.

West Germany

At a meeting which ended on August 30, 1968, a gathering of twenty-two heads of dioceses and over forty auxiliary bishops worked out this declaration which was published on September 11:

"He who thinks that it is permissible for him to deviate in his private theory and practice from a non-infallible teaching of the Church authority—such a case is conceivable in principle—must question his conscience soberly and critically whether he can justify this before God . . .

"The answer must be sought and found by them through conscientious examination based on objective norm and criteria. The concrete way to responsible parenthood should not offend the dignity of the

human person or endanger the harmonious fruitful
love of marriage . . .

"Pastors will respect in their work, especially in the
administration of the sacraments, the decisions of
conscience of the believers made in the awareness of
their responsibility. We will endeavor, working
together with priests and lay people, to seek practical ways for the pastoral care of the married."

Australia

On September 23, 1968, the Australian hierarchy
declared:

"Because the encyclical is not an infallible judgment,
it is conceivable that some Catholics will believe that
they cannot accept this ruling.

"Whoever is an expert in this field and came to a
conviction different from that of the encyclical after
serious self-examination and not because of an emotional reaction is allowed to follow his conviction.
Such a person does not sin if he is ready to continue
examining the situation and otherwise shows
respect and loyalty to the Church."

England

The hierarchy of England and Wales issued their statement on September 25, 1968. It read in part:

"A particular difficulty faces those who, after serious
thought and prayer, cannot as yet understand or be
fully convinced of the doctrines as laid down. This is
not surprising, in view of the discussions of recent

years which have resulted in the present controversy.

"The Holy Father realizes what difficulties face married people. . . . The encyclical makes no sweeping condemnations. There is no threat of damnation.

"Far from being excluded from the sacraments those in difficulties are invited to receive them more frequently."

Italy

In the statement of the presidential council of the Italian Bishops' Conference, addressed to Pope Paul VI, and published in *L'Osservatore Romano* on September 15, 1968, there is a strong and apparently unconditional endorsement of *Humanae Vitae*.

Two points, however, constitute definite qualifications. The first is a distinction clearly made between those who use contraception for selfish motives only, and others who do so because of the "difficulty, at times very serious, in which they find themselves, that of reconciling the demands of responsible parenthood with those of mutual love." The text continues:

"In such a case, in fact, their behavior, although not in conformity with the Christian norm, cannot surely be equated in its serious importance with that which might spring solely from motives vitiated by egotism and hedonism."

Canada

The Canadian hierarchy, in its declaration of September 27, 1968, upheld the right of Catholics, after a sincere self-examination regarding their true motives, to follow their consciences in the use of contraceptives and to receive Holy Communion without going to confession, thus implying, as did the bishops of England and Wales, that such people are not in a state of serious sin.

"We must appreciate the difficulty experienced by contemporary man in understanding and appropriating some of the points of this encyclical and we must make every effort to learn from the insights of Catholic scientists and intellectuals who are of undoubted loyalty to Christian truth, to the Church and to the authority of the Holy See.

"Since they are not denying any point of divine and Catholic faith or rejecting the teaching authority of the Church, these Catholics should not be considered, or consider themselves, shut off from the body of the faithful.

"But they should remember that their good faith will be dependent on a sincere self-examination to determine the true motives and grounds for such suspension of assent and on continued effort to understand and deepen their knowledge of the teaching of the Church.

". . . In accord with the accepted principles of moral theology, if these persons (who are involved in conflicts of duties) have tried sincerely but without success to pursue a line of conduct in keeping with the given directives, they may be safely assured that whoever honestly chooses that course which seems right to him does so in good conscience."

Pope Paul VI seems to have approved this declaration. In a letter, quoted in the November 13, 1968 issue of the *National Catholic Reporter,* Archbishop Emmanuele Clarizio, Apostolic Delegate to Canada at the time wrote to Bishop Alexander Carter, President of the Canadian Bishops' Conference:

> "Now I am happy to notify your excellency that his eminence Cardinal Amleto Cicognani, Secretary of State to His Holiness, has just communicated to the delegation that the Holy Father Pope Paul VI has taken cognizance of the document with satisfaction."

Scandinavia

In a statement issued October 17, 1968, the six bishops of Denmark, Finland, Norway, and Sweden wrote the following:

> ". . . if someone, from weighty and well-considered reasons, cannot become convinced by the argumentation of the encyclical, it has always been conceded that he is allowed to have a different view from that presented in a non-infallible statement of the Church. No one should be considered a bad Catholic because he is of such a dissenting opinion."

France

The French bishops' pastoral note on *Humanae Vitae* was issued at their plenary assembly in Lourdes in November 1968. Like the other declarations of national hierarchies, it supports the encyclical in principle. However, there were reservations:

"Contraception can never be good. It is always a disorder, but this disorder is not always culpable."

"No one is unaware of the spiritual agonies in which sincere husbands and wives struggle, particularly when the observance of natural rhythms does not succeed 'in providing a sufficiently secure basis for the regulation of birth.' "

"On this subject, we shall simply recall the constant teaching of morality: when one has an alternative choice (between conflicting) duties and, whatever may be the decision, evil cannot be avoided, traditional wisdom makes provision for seeking before God that which, in the circumstances, is the greater duty. Husband and wife will decide at the end of a common reflection carried out with all the care which their conjugal vocation requires."

This is the principle of twofold effect.

United States

An early and almost unconditional endorsement of *Humanae Vitae* by the American hierarchy received strong opposition from a considerable number of professional theologians. This caused the American bishops to publish on November 15, 1968, a Pastoral Letter entitled "Human Life in Our Day." Its general intent was the defense of life and the condemnation of the use of sexuality for selfish motives. This letter departed from their earlier declaration by mentioning the principle of licit dissent in matters concerned with the non-infallible teachings of the Church. It also contained a surprising statement that rejected the principle of biological necessity, which had been invoked in the encyclical as the foundation of the "natural law" argument. This was the wording of that passage:

> "In its emphasis on the virtues of fidelity and hope, so essential to the prophetic witness of the family, Christian sexual morality derives therefore, not from the inviolability of generative biology, but ultimately from the sanctity of life itself and the nobility of human sexuality. . . .

> "There exists in the Church a lawful freedom of inquiry and of thought and also general norms of licit dissent."

Perhaps the most important passage was this one:

> "In the final analysis, conscience is inviolable and no person is to be forced to act in a manner contrary to his/ her conscience—as the moral tradition of the Church attests."

All these declarations have in common a deep respect for the authority of the Holy Father, together with the firm expression of the primacy of conscience in the practical decisions of daily life.

In the 1970s there was a controversy in the Catholic press concerning the internal forum. Could you describe and clarify what happened?

A bishop in the northwest of the United States developed procedures in his diocese for granting official permission to individuals in non-canonical marriages to return to the sacraments. It was a sincere pastoral effort to bring peace of soul to many deserving couples. It was also an attempt to keep the distance between the external forum and the internal forum from widening further.

Was it the public nature of the procedure that Rome objected to?

Yes. The validity of the internal forum of conscience was not at issue. Conscience is a matter of moral and sacramental theology, not canon law. What the Holy See objected to was basically the same thing they criticized in the case of the three German bishops in 1995. They don't want bishops circumventing the tribunal by creating an administrative procedure which undermines the judicial procedure. To do so is to make a new law. Only the supreme lawmaker, the pope, can enact canon law. The rulings of ecumenical councils are another matter; here he works in collaboration with the college of bishops.

What happened in the United States in the 1970s was this: An official letter came from the Holy See to Cardinal Krol, who was the president of the American hierarchy at that time. The Holy See ordered a stop to the bishops' practice of allowing couples in non-canonical marriages to receive Holy Communion. Krol sent the letter to all the bishops.

Very soon afterward, the bishop who had begun the practice stopped it. It was my impression that no one was publicly reprimanded. Rome didn't want a new custom developing which would put aside the procedural laws of the Code. This incident did not address the conscience or the private thoughts of individuals. No priests were contacted or forbidden to absolve in these complex cases.

In 1965, I wrote an article on this question in *Commonweal* magazine recommending that the laity follow their consciences in these difficult marriage cases. Cardinal Krol wrote me a friendly letter telling me about his doctoral dissertation in canon law. Basically, his conclusion was that couples in non-canonical second marriages could live together provided that they lived as brother and sister.

The idea of having no sexual relations might be possible for some, but the vast majority of married people caught in this dilemma have not been able to accept it. I thanked him for his letter, expressed my reservations, and never heard from him again.

What if the first marriage was a true marriage? The love just died and the couple drifted apart. Can this be the basis of an internal forum solution?

No. Once you say there is no doubt about the validity of the first marriage you admit it has binding power. What can one do in that situation? People move on with their lives as best they can. They stay in the Catholic Church without receiving the sacraments, or they leave the Church and join another Christian denomination, or they remain unchurched. Some enter brother-sister marriages.

Marriage is only ended by the death of one party, but there are other kinds of death that terminate a *de facto* marriage. Emotional death will occur when one party expresses hatred for the other, and leaves to find a new spouse. The abandoned party may have given everything to make the marriage work, but to no avail. When this happens, we need to treat the victim with great kindness. Christ gave us a clear example of his charity when he met the Samaritan woman. She had lived with six husbands. He was courteous to her, even though it was forbidden by law for a Jew to speak to a Samaritan. Jesus not only spoke to her, he told her that he was the Messiah, and chose her to announce his Messianic mission to her entire village. After the people of the village came out to see Jesus, they told the woman, "We no longer believe because of your word; for we have heard for ourselves, and we know that this is truly the savior of the world" (John 4:4-42).

In this Gospel, Jesus takes a kindly attitude toward this multiply married divorcee. He accepts her with no sign of reproach which tells us that God's love is not cut off from anyone, especially not from someone who is genuinely trying to be good. However, as long as one's true husband or true wife is still alive, one cannot be married officially in the Church without an annulment. That's why it's important to seek canonical help to determine if the former union is really a true and valid marriage.

Many people refuse to go to the tribunal because they have heard horror stories about the treatment they will receive.

Yes, it's true but these stories can be highly exaggerated. The tribunal personnel are good men and women who only want to help. Past injustices have created deep suspicions I admit, but for the most part things are different today. I would disagree with those who want to take the easy way out by going to their pastor and asking for re-admittance to the sacraments on the basis of conscience without ever having approached the tribunal.

Do you foresee any major developments in canonical thought on these issues in the next five years?

Not in five years, but jurisprudence is still developing, even within the Roman Rota. This might lead to an expansion of the grounds on which marriages may be declared invalid and a simplification of the procedural law. It is my hope that we move in the direction of a more pastoral approach. The current court procedures can be made less legalistic and less formal. I would like to see a panel of judges hear each case so as to resolve it within one month.

How were the cases of abandoned spouses handled in the early Church?

There was a precedent in the Celtic penitential books of the fifth, sixth, and seventh centuries, which contain references to pastoral solutions in marriage cases based on the Eastern Church's concept of *oikonomia*. This was a way of tempering the harsh impact of the law. In the commentary of the new *Code of Canon Law, oikonomia* is described as "a hidden power in the Church, undefinable, that comes into play in rare and insoluble cases." This is not exactly the same as *epieikeia* which is justice beyond the law. *Oikonomia* pertains to the economy of salvation within the Church. *Epieikeia* puts fairness and justice first, above the strict application of the law if there is a conflict.

In Asia Minor there were instances where bishops resolved the marriage cases of abandoned spouses. For example, the wife of a sailor was left with five children when her husband went off to sea and never returned. After living alone for a long time with no means of support, a suitor asked her to marry him. Since she was already married and her husband was not confirmed as dead, she asked the bishop what she should do. Her first marriage was presumed to be valid and indissoluble, but after due consideration, the bishop invoked the principle of *oikonomia,* and simply allowed her to remarry. Many other bishops took similar actions in those centuries.

Confronting human weakness, these local bishops permitted something that was canonically improper, but pastorally reasonable.

Another example of this principle occurred in the United States during the 1940s, when the bishops of Chicago faced the problem of converting the African American community. The parents of black children in our parochial schools approached the pastors asking to become Catholic. Up until then the pastors had been turning away those who were living in invalid marriages. Legally, they could not accept them as active members in the Church without an annulment. Many of them had been involved in an earlier marriage, and there was little hope of resolving the problem through the marriage tribunal.

The pastors asked the local hierarchy for a pastoral solution, namely that the "marriage in possession" be considered the valid marriage. The request was granted. It was decided that these parents, who had been in previous marriages, would be admitted into the Church anyway. This pastoral decision brought hundreds of black families into the Church and created a strong Black Catholic presence in Chicago.

Canonically the solution was illogical, but pastorally, it was a wise decision. There's a good chance that most of the earlier marriages could have been annulled in an ecclesiastical court anyway, but we'll never really know.

Those of us who are involved in the tribunal system are trying to protect the indissolubility of marriage. Society needs that protection to stabilize family life. At the same time, we want to witness to the mercy of the Lord. It isn't easy trying to balance the two.

I admire and respect everyone who is working in this ministry. Having been a Judicial Vicar, a presiding judge and an appeal court judge for over 40 years, I know how conscientiously my colleagues work to help people get through the tragedy of a broken marriage. Striving for justice tempered with mercy, they are outstanding in their faith, hope and charity.

If you are in need of pastoral help don't be afraid to bring your case to the tribunal. There are many good men and women eager to help you.

CHAPTER 5

Where Does the Church Stand with You?

ONE of the greatest mistakes made by a Church tribunal occurred when St. Joan of Arc was condemned as a witch. This erroneous decision enabled the English civil authorities to burn her at the stake. On the night before she died, she uttered these memorable words: "I love the Church, I will always love the Church, because for me the Church is Jesus Christ." Joan saw the Church as the Mystical Body of Christ. In spite of the great error which took her life, she forgave the Church from her heart.

Terrible mistakes can be made by individual members of the Church, but the Church still remains the Body of Christ. There have been many tragic stories related to Church tribunals and I make no excuses for them. I simply hold up Joan of Arc as an heroic model of forgiveness.

So many good people have been hurt by the Church in the past. If you are one of them, I beg for your forgiveness on behalf of the Church. Please try to get this painful experience behind you and focus on God's infinite love. He wants to heal you and take away the emotional pain.

In the beginning of this book, I raised the question: Where do you stand with the Church? Now I would like to reverse the question: Where does the Church stand with you? Do you want to come back? If so, do it! Come home.

If you do nothing and allow the guilt, the pain, and the anger to fester beneath the surface, your emotional life will suffer. You can change that. You can decide to let the Church minister to you.

I remember a couple in an invalid marriage who reconciled with the Church in time to celebrate their fiftieth wedding anniversary. They had the courage to pursue that elusive goal, and they succeeded. You may not have far to go. Remember, if you are divorced, that does not mean you are separated from the Church. No matter what anyone may say, you are still a Catholic. The door is not closed to you.

There have been so many painful cases that I shudder to think of them. I recall one woman whose husband left her after only a few years of marriage. He said he felt trapped and needed to find himself. He walked away and eventually got a divorce. Unfortunately, someone told her that she could no longer receive Holy Communion unless she got an annulment. This was completely untrue. She went to her parish priest, but he didn't even take the time to listen to her story. He just gave her an application for an annulment, and told her to complete the forms. She carried those papers in her purse for three years, all the time thinking she couldn't receive the Eucharist. She couldn't find the courage to fill the papers out, and she couldn't bear to throw them away. It was tragic because during those three years she really believed that she was excommunicated. Fortunately, she now knows that it is all right to receive Holy Communion when you are separated or divorced and have not remarried. The Church never rejected her, but she was treated shabbily by a priest, who didn't take the time to listen.

If you gain anything from this book perhaps it will be the courage to seek out a kind priest who will help you to break down the barriers that separate you from God and the Church. If one priest doesn't treat you with kindness, try another. There is someone out there waiting to help you. Find that person and your life will improve immeasurably.

In the process, you will probably dredge up some painful memories, but it's worth the effort. Sometimes, the only way to heal a festering wound is to cut it open and let the poison drain out. In spite of the initial pain, it will be a healing process for you. If you do nothing at all, you will only prolong the pain.

When I encounter people who have been away from the Church for a long time, I gently invite them back to the sacrament of Reconciliation.

In the privacy of confession, Jesus Christ ministers to you through the ministry of the priest. You can say things to a priest that you would not say to anyone else. The priest is in a position to help you put your unhappy experiences into perspective. A great weight will be lifted from your shoulders and your spiritual healing will begin.

I know how frightened and anxious some people feel about the confessional. I try to make it as easy as possible for them—especially if they have been away from the

Church for a long time. This is what I do when I have such a penitent. We go through the Ten Commandments in order to make a general confession. All they have to do is say yes or no, as I mention each Commandment.

The First Commandment: *I am the Lord thy God. Thou shalt not put false gods before me.* I start by asking if they ever joined any other religions, or if they have ever engaged in occult or superstitious practices, etc.

The Second Commandment: *Thou shalt not take the name of the Lord thy God in vain.* I ask how often they swear or use God's name irreverently.

The Third Commandment: *Remember to keep holy the Sabbath.* I ask if they miss Mass frequently.

The Fourth Commandment: *Honor thy father and thy mother.* I ask if they've been good to their parents. We talk about it if there have been problems in that area.

When we get to the Fifth Commandment, *Thou shalt not kill,* I ask if they ever shot anyone while robbing a bank, and they usually laugh. Then I ask if they have ever had an abortion, or in the case of a man, if he has ever been responsible for putting a woman in the position to have an abortion. This guilt is something that sacramental absolution can ease. I tell them that it is all behind them now, and I reassure them that the Lord will forgive them. All they have to do is ask for forgiveness and trust in God's mercy and love. God's love is caring for their infant.

Then we move on to the Sixth Commandment: *Thou shalt not commit adultery.* I ask if there are any sexual sins they want to mention. Oddly enough, most people don't even mention that they are in an invalid marriage, which is the basis of the whole problem. They obviously, don't think of it as a sin.

Next, the Seventh Commandment: *Thou shalt not steal.* I ask if they have ever stolen anything, or exploited people for profit.

The Eighth Commandment: *Thou shalt not bear false witness against thy neighbor.* I ask if they ever lied to hurt anyone.

Then we conclude with the last two commandments: *Thou shalt not covet.* Coveting your neighbor's spouse or your neighbor's goods involves the sins of lust or envy.

When we're through, I ask if there's anything else they want to talk about. I listen, and when they have finished talking, I try to put them at ease. I ask them to renew their good intentions and together we thank God for his love and mercy. I remind them that sometimes we stray from the Lord, but now it's time to come home.

Often I tell them that their penance will include all the pain and suffering they've endured over the years since their last confession. I might also ask them to put a few coins in the poor box in reparation for their sins. It is important to remember the poor of the world. St. Peter said that charity overcomes a multitude of sins.

Next, I ask them to make an act of contrition. Some people don't recall the exact formula they learned as a child, but I assure them that it doesn't matter. They can just tell God they are sorry in their own words. Then I give them absolution and I follow up with this prayer:

"May the passion of Our Lord Jesus Christ, the merits of the Blessed Virgin Mary and all the Saints, and also whatever good you do or suffering you endure, be cause for the remission of your sins, the increase of grace, and the gift of everlasting life."

Most priests are loving and gentle in the confessional. There is the occasional priest, who might be a bit rigid. If you are coming back after a long time, you need to find a priest who will help and comfort you. You are not the greatest sinner in the world even if you think you are. You have the right to select any priest you want for your confession. You also have the right to walk out of the confessional if a priest treats you in a way that upsets you. I'm not saying that a priest shouldn't challenge you, but if you feel that he completely misunderstands what you are saying, or if he treats you in an unkind way, you have a right to leave the confessional and find another priest.

If you have been away from the Church for a long time, please have the courage to take the next step. If you are in an invalid or uncanonical marriage, ask a priest about your options for an annulment. If for some reason you cannot obtain an annulment through no fault of your own, then learn more about the internal forum solution. It may be a viable option in your situation.

Millions of Catholics gave up on the Catholic Church a long time ago. Some joined another Church. It may have been the best thing they could do. I thank God there was a comforting Christian community to receive them. If you are one of those people, perhaps the fact that you are reading this book indicates that you may still yearn to return to your Catholic roots.

This is an issue you will have to face with courage. I have known Catholics, who were good Lutherans or good Episcopalians for years. They raised their children in those churches, and were well served by their ministers. Yet they are still carrying a deep-seated desire to return to the Catholic Church and receive Holy Communion. If you are such a person, I want to assure you, if you don't already know it, that God's love for you has never wavered.

Ultimately, all of us will be judged on how well we have loved God and neighbor. Read the Gospel of St. Matthew, Chapter 25, and you'll understand what the final judgment will be like. You will not be asked how many times you were married. You will be asked how hard you tried to be a loving person.

No matter what, don't put yourself down. You are a good person trying to be better. The Lord himself wants you to trust his love. God's love is unchanging.

In baptism God sealed his life to yours. You became a temple of the Holy Spirit, a member of the Body of Christ. That seal was an indelible, permanent character. God will never let you go, but neither will he take your freedom away. You can walk away from him if you choose, but he will constantly try to draw you back to himself.

In my book, *God Delights in You* (Alba House), I tried to describe God's love in a variety of ways. The image I like best is that of a young mother with her precious infant. She loves her child even though the baby wakes her in the middle of the night. She loves that child when he soils his diapers and spits up. No matter what the circumstances, the mother's love is attentive, full of affection and ready to serve. God's love is infinitely more powerful than a mother's love.

What's my point? It is simply this: God not only loves you, he delights in loving you. Even when your life gets messy, he never stops loving you. You are closer to God right now than you are to your own heartbeat.

If you sense that the Lord is leading you back to the Catholic Church, why not go with the flow. If you meet obstacles, walk around them, climb over them, but don't let them stop you. Focus on God's unchanging love and trust him. The Holy Spirit will guide you all the way home.

Meanwhile, I promise to remember you at Mass and in prayer.

God bless you.

OTHER BOOKS OF INTEREST

GROWING IN FAITH WHEN A CATHOLIC MARRIAGE FAILS
For Divorced or Separated Catholics and Those Who Minister with Them
Antoinette Bosco

Building on the experience of other divorced and remarried Catholics, Ms. Bosco shares her extensive knowledge of Church law and the process of annulment with deep compassion and understanding. A source of hope, encouragement and support for divorced Catholics and a healing resource for those who minister in the Catholic community.

No. RP 748/04   ISBN 978-1-933066-04-2   **$8.95**

DISCERNMENT
Seeking God in Every Situation
Rev. Chris Aridas

"This is a book to cherish. It should be read slowly and prayerfully. Then it can be re-read again and again providing special nourishment for those who take their spiritual journey seriously." —*Robert E. Lauder*

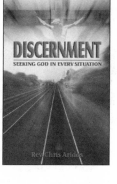

. . . a spiritual road map for decision-making in the Spirit. It provides inspiration to desire to follow God as well as simple, sensible and direct guidance to assist the seeker to follow God's will in their everyday life."
—*Sr. Nancy Kellar*

No. RP 194/04   ISBN 978-1-933066-88-6   **$8.95**

A PARTY OF ONE
Meditations for Those Who Live Alone
Joni Woelfel

Using each day's brief reflection, probing question and pertinent quote by Adolfo Quezada, this book will comfort and empower those living alone to take ownership of their life, confident of being guided and upheld by God.

No. RP 744/04   ISBN 978-1-933066-01-1   **$5.95**

www.catholicbookpublishing.com

OTHER BOOKS OF INTEREST

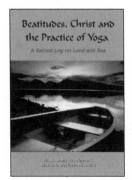

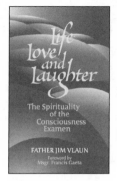
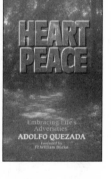
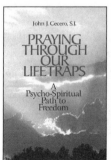

OTHER BOOKS OF INTEREST

GRACE NOTES
Embracing the Joy of Christ in a Broken World
Lorraine V. Murray

"... will help you to see what we should be able to see naturally, but for some reason it takes grace to recognize grace! Her book is well named."

—Fr. Richard Rohr, O.F.M.

No. RP 154/04 ISBN 978-1-878718-69-3   **$9.95**

THE EDGE OF GREATNESS
Empowering Meditations for Life
Joni Woelfel

"Here is a woman whose courageous and passionate spirit has enabled her to step over the edge of greatness. She knows how to walk on water, because she has kept her eyes on the One who created the waters. Read this book and be blessed."   **—Macrina Wiederkehr, OSB**

No. RP 134/04 ISBN 978-1-878718-93-8   **$9.95**

WOMANSOUL
Letters of Encouragement and Possibility
Pat Duffy, OP

"... challenges without threatening or judging and encourages readers to step bravely toward the shining truth that each is a treasure cherished by God. Armed with that reality a woman can begin to reach into the infinity of her own soul."   **—Liz O'Connor, Editor**

No. RP 152/04 ISBN 978-1-878718-68-6   **$7.95**

FEASTS OF LIFE
Recipes from Nana's Wooden Spoon
Father Jim Vlaun

"Filled with wonderful stories and even better-sounding recipes ... The dishes are easy to make and don't require fancy ingredients. Includes a prayer for grace, a cooking equivalents table and a cross-referenced index."   **—Crux of the News**

No. RP 168/04 ISBN 978-1-878718-76-1   **$12.95**

www.catholicbookpublishing.com

OTHER BOOKS OF INTEREST

LOVING YOURSELF FOR GOD'S SAKE
Adolfo Quezada

This exquisite book of meditations gently directs the reader to see the gift of self in an entirely new and beautiful light. It presents a spirituality of self-love not based on narcissism, but as a response to the divine invitation to self-nurturing.

No. RP 720/04 ISBN 978-1-878718-35- 8   **$5.95**

HEALING THE WOUNDS OF EMOTIONAL ABUSE
The Journey Worth the Risk
Nancy Benvenga

". . . offers readers both sound principles of guidance and hope-filled resources for prayer and healing."
—Spiritual Book News

". . . strikes the perfect balance between professional insight and personal witness. . . . well researched, highly readable, warmly personal and a practical godsend for those who struggle with emotional abuse."
—Msgr. James P. Lisante

No. RP 580/04 ISBN 978-1-878718-30-3   **$6.95**

SOMETIMES I HAVEN'T GOT A PRAYER
. . . And Other "Real" Catholic Adventures
Mary Kavanagh Sherry

. . . down-to-earth, even extremely funny, and filled with insights born of love and lighthearted determination to be a growing yet faithful believer committed to Catholicism. . . . provides excellent questions for reflection."   **—Dominican Vision**

No. RP 174/04 ISBN 978-1-878718-79-2   **$8.95**

www.catholicbookpublishing.com

Additional Titles Published by Resurrection Press, a Catholic Book Publishing Imprint

A Rachel Rosary *Larry Kupferman*	$4.50
A Season in the South *Marci Alborghetti*	$10.95
Blessings All Around *Dolores Leckey*	$8.95
Catholic Is Wonderful *Mitch Finley*	$4.95
Discernment *Chris Aridas*	$8.95
Edge of Greatness *Joni Woelfel*	$9.95
Feasts of Life *Jim Vlaun*	$12.95
Grace Notes *Lorraine Murray*	$9.95
Healing through the Mass *Robert DeGrandis, SSJ*	$9.95
Healing Your Grief *Ruthann Williams, OP*	$7.95
Heart Peace *Adolfo Quezada*	$9.95
How Shall We Become Holy? *Mary Best*	$6.95
How Shall We Celebrate? *Lorraine Murray*	$6.95
How Shall We Pray? *James Gaffney*	$5.95
The Joy of Being an Altar Server *Joseph Champlin*	$5.95
The Joy of Being a Bereavement Minister *Nancy Stout*	$5.95
The Joy of Being a Catechist *Gloria Durka*	$4.95
The Joy of Being a Eucharistic Minister *Mitch Finley*	$5.95
The Joy of Being a Lector *Mitch Finley*	$5.95
The Joy of Being an Usher *Gretchen Hailer, RSHM*	$5.95
The Joy of Marriage Preparation *McDonough/Marinelli*	$5.95
The Joy of Music Ministry *J.M. Talbot*	$6.95
The Joy of Praying the Psalms *Nancy de Flon*	$5.95
The Joy of Praying the Rosary *James McNamara*	$5.95
The Joy of Preaching *Rod Damico*	$6.95
The Joy of Teaching *Joanmarie Smith*	$5.95
The Joy of Worshiping Together *Rod Damico*	$5.95
Lessons for Living from the 23rd Psalm *Victor Parachin*	$6.95
Lights in the Darkness *Ave Clark, O.P.*	$8.95
Loving Yourself for God's Sake *Adolfo Quezada*	$5.95
Magnetized by God *Robert E. Lauder*	$8.95
Meditations for Survivors of Suicide *Joni Woelfel*	$8.95
Mercy Flows *Rod Damico*	$9.95
Mother Teresa *Eugene Palumbo, S.D.B.*	$5.95
Mourning Sickness *Keith Smith*	$8.95
Our Grounds for Hope *Fulton J. Sheen*	$7.95
Personally Speaking *Jim Lisante*	$8.95
Power of One *Jim Lisante*	$9.95
Praying the Lord's Prayer with Mary *Muto/vanKaam*	$8.95
5-Minute Miracles *Linda Schubert*	$4.95
Sabbath Moments *Adolfo Quezada*	$6.95
Season of New Beginnings *Mitch Finley*	$4.95
Sometimes I Haven't Got a Prayer *Mary Sherry*	$8.95
St. Katharine Drexel *Daniel McSheffery*	$12.95
What He Did for Love *Francis X. Gaeta*	$5.95
Woman Soul *Pat Duffy, OP*	$7.95
You Are My Beloved *Mitch Finley*	$10.95

For a free catalog call 1-800-892-6657

www.catholicbookpublishing.com